The Musical Languages of Elliott Carter

Elliott Carter

The Musical Languages of Elliott Carter

by Charles Rosen

Music Division   Research Services

Library of Congress   Washington   1984

780.92
C245
DR722m

84-1827

Library of Congress Cataloging in Publication Data

Rosen, Charles, 1927–
    The musical languages of Elliott Carter.

    Bibliography: p.
    Includes: A guide to Elliott Carter research materials
at the Library of Congress Music Division/by Morgan
Cundiff.
    1. Carter, Elliott, 1908– . 2. Carter, Elliott,
1908– —Bibliography. 3. Library of Congress.
Music Division—Catalogs. I. Cundiff, Morgan. Guide
to Elliott Carter research materials at the Library of
Congress Music Division. 1984. II. Title.
ML410.C3293R7 1984   780'.92'4   84–3851
ISBN O-8444-0449-7

For sale by the Superintendent of Documents, U.S. Government Printing Office
Washington, D.C. 20402

Contents

Elliott Carter

Foreword

As part of its celebration of Elliott Carter's seventieth birthday, the Library of Congress invited Charles Rosen to perform the composer's Piano Sonata (1946). It seemed fitting that Mr. Rosen—being both a preeminent interpreter of Elliott Carter's piano music and a distinguished writer and lecturer—be asked to deliver a lecture on the work he was to perform. The Piano Sonata marks a turning point in Carter's composition method (his earlier works having been written in a more accessible idiom). Moreover, it has become increasingly popular among pianists and audiences alike, and it makes an excellent introduction to the works of a composer whose very name evokes a response of fear among some who would like to feel comfortable with modern music but are frightened by the complexity of Carter's music. The lecture was delivered extemporaneously and with many musical examples before the concert on October 7, 1978, and was presented under the auspices of the Louis Charles Elson Memorial Fund in the Music Division. As plans to prepare this lecture for publication proceeded, various additions were proposed by the author and others, and the resulting book is the most extensive publication to have originated, so far, from an Elson lecture.

Louis Charles Elson (1848-1920) was a distinguished author, composer, and editor. He taught at the New England Conservatory of Music and was music editor for Boston newspapers. In 1945 his widow, Bertha L. Elson, established the fund through a bequest, to sponsor lectures in memory of her husband. Many of them have been published by the Library since the first lecture in 1946.

Mr. Rosen's lecture was first transcribed, and then edited (with much valuable assistance from Morgan Cundiff) and rewritten by Mr. Rosen. Meanwhile, we decided to include Mr. Cundiff's extensive guide to Elliott Carter research materials in the Library's Music Division, together with his bibliography of writings by and about the composer. Then, it was suggested that a previously published essay by Mr. Rosen that had appeared in the *New York Review of Books* (February 22, 1973) would well complement his Elson lecture. It concerns some of Mr. Rosen's experiences as pianist performing Carter's Double Concerto and discovering the reasons for, and methods of overcoming some of its formidable difficulties.

In April 1983, as the final touches were being put on a publication that we intended to be a seventy-fifth birthday tribute to Elliott Carter, I made a phone call to the composer concerning some detail or other and learned that at that moment he was being interviewed by Mr. Rosen for the B.B.C. The interview went so well that we decided that it, too, should be published. In the interview, subjects discussed in Mr. Rosen's earlier two essays are developed further by the composer himself. These include not only purely musical matters, such as the relationship between sonority and rhythm, but the human side of Carter's music: his sometimes programmatic ideas about his pieces, his idea of instruments as persons.

While the transcript of the interview was being edited, Mr. Cundiff noted that his bibliography was already becoming outdated and he generously expanded it to include some more recent entries.

Here, at last, are both Elliott Carter's seventieth and seventy-fifth birthday offerings from the Library of Congress. Indeed, there is no occasion on which such illuminating discussions of the works of a great composer—works that, in the composer's own words, are "difficult to some people, and profoundly exciting to others"—would not seem appropriate.

JON NEWSOM
Assistant Chief
Music Division

The Musical Languages of Elliott Carter

by Charles Rosen

I would like to begin this lecture with an apology. It is an odd thing for me to play Elliott Carter's Piano Sonata with the score since I used to perform it from memory. But I had two frightening experiences with this piece. One occurred on my playing it for the first time. Having already prepared the Sonata for a tour in Germany, I was unexpectedly asked to play it at a festival of contemporary music in Brussels. Just before I walked out on the stage the concert manager said, "Isn't it nice the composer has come to hear you play this piece?" Never having performed it before, I was, of course, terrified, but I got through it without any problems and played it many times after that, always by heart. Then Mr. Carter asked me to play it in New York at a concert of contemporary music and just before I walked out on the stage, one of the other musicians on the program said, "My God! You're not going to play *that* piece without the music are you?" So, of course, I forgot a page in the fugue. Ever since then I have used the music to calm my nerves, although that also has its problems: since I know the work by heart, I generally lose my place when I try to look at the score.

My apology is prompted by the common belief in the difficulty of contemporary music, and which is epitomized by a wonderful story told by Eduard Steuermann. A man came to him after a concert and said, "Mr. Steuermann, I've written a book to prove that one cannot play twelve-tone music by heart." Steuermann replied, "But I play it by heart all the time." The man was silent for a moment, but then brightened up and said, "You're lying."

On the subject of the real, as opposed to the imaginary difficulties of contemporary music, I recall speaking to Carter some years ago about the difficulty of composing for the piano after about 1920. I remarked on how much easier it must have been to be a composer in the eighteenth and nineteenth centuries, for then one had all kinds of scales, arpeggios, and commonly accepted devices with which to write. I was thinking of those long cadential passages that appear even in the finest pieces by Mozart, passages which one could almost transfer unaltered from one piece to another. (When practicing one of the B-flat concertos—K. 450—I have actually found myself absentmindedly playing another one of them—K. 595.) Carter replied that composition was not only more difficult now, but that every time one wrote a piece it seemed as if one had to reinvent a language in which to write it. A number of composers have felt this way, but it seems to me that no one has been quite so successful with this kind of invention as Carter; and I would like to discuss why this is so.

This lecture preceded Mr. Rosen's performance of Elliott Carter's Piano Sonata in the Library's Coolidge Auditorium on October 7, 1978.

1

For me, the Piano Sonata is the ideal beginning for such a discussion, since, for one thing, it is the only solo piano piece that Carter has written.[1] For the purpose of illustration here, it is all I have. There are, of course, the two great works with solo piano: the Double Concerto for Harpsichord and Piano with Two Chamber Orchestras, and the more recent Piano Concerto that requires a large orchestra. But, besides offering the convenience of being a solo work, the Sonata has special significance. Composed in 1945 and 1946, it bears witness to the moment when Carter started inventing his musical language, and it does so in a way that is extraordinarily interesting.

The concept of music as a language needs elucidation. Just as in everyday speech we build sentences not syllable by syllable or even word by word, but often by stringing together entire stock phrases, there have been times in the history of music when composers have had musical materials similar to the stock phrases we use in verbal language. A group of Beethoven sketches seemed at first inexplicable: they consisted solely of different kinds of figuration made up of various patterns of scales and arpeggios. Then it was suggested, quite rightly I think, that they were his personal repertory of formulas for improvising at the keyboard. The practice of writing out such things and memorizing them is certainly no novelty. Musical stock phrases can be gathered and used whether one is improvising or composing. They need not be very long; they can just be a measure or so. But that still provides the composer with whole phrases or blocks of material that he can use in his piece.

However, the use of such procedures has become difficult in our times for reasons too complex to discuss here. A great many composers have tried to invent what might be called systematic blocks. In a way, that is what Schoenberg's method of composing with twelve tones and its later systemizations provide: a repertory exactly as Beethoven had compiled for improvisaton—a repertory for a composition. Once you devise a twelve-tone row, you have many preestablished sequences of notes from which you can choose as material for your piece. A number of composers, Carter in particular, have felt that twelve-tone or serial systems as they are sometimes conceived (not always as they are used) tyrannize the process of composition, and they have rejected serialism for their own work. Carter is perhaps the only major composer of our time who has never even tried to write a serial work.

I should add that Carter makes thousands of sketches while writing a piece. The nature of sketching is sometimes misunderstood because for every composer the process and purpose are quite different. In some cases it is a working towards the final piece (and some of Carter's sketches do just that). But once Carter has the idea for a piece, most of the sketches serve as a kind of repertory. That is, having invented the idea of the piece, he then starts inventing the vocabulary of the piece. Of course, much of this vocabulary is thrown away just as a writer rejects many possible formulations every time he writes.

2

The Piano Sonata is, as I have said, the first of Carter's pieces to invent part of its own language. A great deal of the Sonata is still traditional; even so, part of that tradition is a reinvented tradition, as I shall try to show. I would like to start with harmony because I think that this aspect of the Sonata has been neglected while the rhythmic inventions have often been appreciated. Carter's rhythm has, quite rightly, received a great deal of publicity, but in some ways the most extraordinary rhythmic invention is derived from the harmony. (Of course, you can look at it the other way and show how some of the harmonic ideas depend on new conceptions of rhythm.)

Perhaps it would help to reconstruct the situation in 1945 when the Sonata was written. This was a moment when composers were trying to revive the large romantic forms that had been more or less thrown aside by a long neoclassical period that lasted from the 1920s. If we compare Carter's Sonata of 1947 and the Piano Sonata of Samuel Barber, written at the same time, with the sonatas of the 1930s—that is, with the sonatas of Stravinsky, Copland, and Hindemith—we can see an attempt to recover the romantic quality of the piano. The Carter piece remains, I think, the great pianistic achievement of the 1940s; and it has gradually worked its way into the repertoire of a large number of pianists. (Those who want to play a more conservative but romantic style have generally taken up the Ginastera or the Barber Sonatas or one of the late Prokofiev Sonatas.) Carter's Piano Sonata is comparable in its ambition to works of greater dissonance that followed it, such as Boulez's Piano Sonata no. 2, equally neoromantic and equally an attempt to capture a similar grandeur. Boulez's work is based openly on Beethoven's Hammerklavier op. 106; and it is fairly obvious (at least to me, though, I hasten to say, probably not to Mr. Carter) that behind Carter's Sonata there must have been a lingering memory of the Liszt Sonata in B Minor. Particularly the last page of Liszt's sonata is in evidence, and I think that Liszt's striking ending would unconsciously influence any work in B major today. Carter's Sonata has many Lisztian characteristics even though the figuration, insofar as it is traditional (and not much of it is), is derived more from Chopin's music than from anything else.

I should like to start with an anomaly. The Sonata is clearly in B major but the first movement ends on a B-flat.

It is anomalous but not surprising. When heard in context, it is an extraordinarily convincing ending. That is, an A-sharp or B-flat has become a convincing point of cadence for a piece in B.

This anomaly allows me to say that although there are many parts of the piece which are in fact tonal, it is not, for the most part, a strictly tonal piece; that is, it is not tonal in the sense that it employs a system based on the use of a central tonic triad, its dominant, and all the other triads and chords arranged in a hierarchical relation to the tonic. There are, for example, very few uses in this piece of a real dominant-tonic relationship.

In fact, what is even more surprising about the piece is that there are very few triads in root position. (There is one startling tonic triad in root position held for a long time just before the beginning of the development section.) But most of the triads have both the flattened third as well as the major third. It is interesting that when this occurs it never sounds like a mistake; this is not the "wrong-note" style of so much modern music. Elliott Carter himself has observed that some of his early pieces were written in that style—tonal music with a little peppery dissonance thrown in. The flattened third is made to sound like the right note each time that it occurs, and one can explain this by the underlying harmony of the work. Almost all the themes in the pieces are derived from one basic chord, constructed by just piling one fifth on top of another. This is the basic chord of the piece: (B, F#, C#, G#, D# and A#):

There are two curious things about this chord. One is that even in traditional tonal terms it resolves two ways. It resolves to a B-major triad and also resolves convincingly to B-flat. In other words, it is a chord that looks both towards B major and B-flat major. This explains the convincing cadence on B-flat. The second characteristic is that the chord outlines a major seventh and yet sounds stable. This stability arises from the great use made in this work of the harmonics of the piano. Carter himself has said that when he started the piece he wanted to exploit the specific sonority of the piano. One of the things a piano can do is make harmonics, that is, sympathetic vibrations in strings that are not struck, but are held open by the pedal. I do not want you to think, by the way, that the harmonics (or overtones) of the piano are exclusively the kind of isolated sounds like the effect in measures 124 through 129 of the first movement:

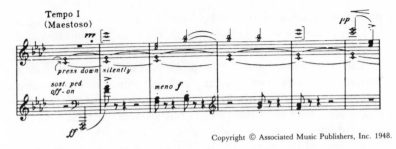

That is one example of the use of harmonics. There are others. When Chopin begins his Nocturne op. 9, no. 2 it sounds particularly beautiful because the notes are arranged in such a way that the bass note and the inner voices stimulate the overtones of the melody notes and the result is that extraordinarily lyrical sound characteristic of Chopin:

There are certain composers, Chopin and Debussy above all, who exploit this capacity of the piano, and other composers, equally great, who do not, or only do so to a lesser extent. Beethoven, for example, does not exploit sonority as much as Mozart. For Debussy, of course, sonority is placed in the center of the music.

Working with the sonorities of Carter's Piano Sonata taught me something interesting about piano acoustics. I telephoned Mr. Carter one day to tell him that I had remarked that playing a B-natural with considerable force stimulates the B-flat harmonics on the piano but does not stimulate the A-natural. This struck me as odd; although I knew almost nothing about acoustics, I had always understood that the minor seventh is a more powerful harmonic than the major seventh—that is, it occurs earlier in the harmonic series—so it should be much stronger. Mr. Carter's reply to this was, "Perhaps that's just something about your piano. Have you tried it on other pianos?" I was very pleased to see he knew as little about acoustics as I did.

I finally looked it up in a musical dictionary and learned there that in equal temperament the major seventh, and not the minor seventh, is an important overtone and that *the notes of Carter's basic chord are in fact the only harmonics that have any importance in equal temperament.* In other words, when the piece begins with just a B, the rest of the notes of that chord start to vibrate sympathetically with more power than any other notes on the piano. This is almost subliminal, but it certainly works on our sensibilities and obviously worked powerfully on Carter's. I think we can take Carter literally when he says that he tried out the sonorities of the piano, and that the piece eventually emerged from them.

This, I suppose, raises a false problem: the distinction between a conscious, systematic way of writing and an unconscious, unsystematic way. I can hardly believe that any of this is ever completely unconscious. I myself must have been conscious of this when playing the piece, or I would not have been drawn to imagine and try out the possibilities in the overtones of the single note B. We may, however, distinguish between a formulated and an unformulated aesthetic. There is no question, for example, that Schoenberg did not compose his twelve-tone music exclusively by a twelve-tone aesthetic. Similarly, people have tried unsuccessfully to explain the serial technique in *Le Marteau sans Maître*, and Pierre Boulez has admitted that after he wrote the piece, it sounded a little bare so he added some more notes. Of course, that does not imply that these other notes were added unconsciously, or that there were no musical principles involved, even if these were incompletely formulated. In the same way, this feeling for the sonority of the piano, its overtones, and the kinds of harmony that could come out of them is an extraordinary testimony to Carter's sensibility and to his ear.

The main themes of the first movement of Carter's Sonata are very clearly derived from the basic chord, and there is a transposed version for both themes. The chord is built up this way in the transposed version:

This explains the extraordinary sonority in this piece. The A-sharp or B-flat is not a dominant (that is, it does not function in the place of an F-sharp, and only rarely as a leading tone to B), but it does function as a substitute or alternate tonic. This is not in the sense of being a key to which one modulates, but rather as a secondary tonic that acts along with the original tonic and into which the music sometimes dissolves as, for example, in the very beautiful ending of the first movement. The continuous suggestion of a B-flat along with the B-natural explains that frequency of triads with the major and minor thirds together, as the principal overtones of B-flat give one the D-natural along with the D-sharp of the B-major triad. Notice, by the way, that even if all the notes of this basic chord, except the bottom one, are played only as harmonics (that is, held down without being sounded, while the bottom B-natural note is struck), they can still be heard clearly. This, again, is the reason that the chord vibrates so richly even when the notes are actually sounded rather than played only as harmonics. It is from this vibration that the

6

melodies emerge. The greatest passage of all is perhaps the line that begins in measure 15. It unfolds from the basic chord and projects itself all over the piano. This is the musical justification of the very considerable use of harmonics.

The rhythm in the Sonata is related to the harmony in a way that is, I think, very original. A regular beat is traditionally associated with tonality. The dominant-tonic relationships of the music of the eighteenth and nineteenth centuries demanded a regular beat with a bar line. The reason is that, in tonal music, the bar line is determined much more by the harmony than by anything else. The simplest way of defining a bar line in the eighteenth century was by a dominant-tonic cadence in which the tonic chord becomes the first beat of the next measure. This could be used in a very sophisticated fashion; for example, in the unison opening of the third movement of his Symphony no. 93 Haydn contradicts and then immediately confirms this principle:

The placement of implied dominant harmony on the first strong beat goes against the grain and requires a bit of an effort. The result adds great interest and charm to an otherwise ordinary minuet rhythm. Of course, this also determines the phrasing and there are other of Haydn's compositions in which the effect appears as a kind of joke.

With the Piano Sonata Carter to a large extent renounces dominant-tonic harmony, but he does not give up the bar line. Therefore, the bar line must be determined in some other way—by phrasing. The phrasing in the Piano Sonata, and in all of Carter's later pieces, may be called unclassical. The reason for this is very simple. If the bar line is not determined by dominant-tonic harmony, it must be determined by accent.

In other words, one can just rhythmically punch holes in the music at irregular intervals. With classical phrasing the regular metric pulse as well as the harmony pull toward the next measure, while Carter has to supply that kind of pull with rhythmic accents. Take, for example, the phrasing and the accentuation in measures 75 to 85 of the second movement, where the fugue theme begins to emerge.

In classical phrasing the end of the phrase would be diminished with a graceful tapering off. But Carter has marked the phrases crescendo to a last note sforzando. These accented notes are not felt as a downbeat but more as an impulse towards the end of the measure. Although it is notated in 6/8, the rhythm and phrasing of this passage do not strictly follow the bar line.

This originality of phrasing in Carter's music poses one of the hardest problems for a pianist who has never done any of it before. If he tries to phrase the music in the traditional way, the result is rather bland, with almost no dynamic impulse. I am really thinking now not so much of the Piano Sonata, in which there is still a good deal of classical phrasing, but of more recent pieces, such as the Piano Concerto and the Double Concerto for Harpsichord and Piano with Two Chamber Orchestras. In these works it is very difficult for instrumentalists to conceive of a phrasing which goes against much of the training they have been given, but which is absolutely necessary for the music.

The Piano Sonata is notated with bar lines which, unlike those in the later works, still have a strict meaning. There is, however, a continuously changing time signature in the first movement which is slightly concealed by the published version of the work. The manuscript of the first movement shows a variety of meters changing every bar or two—8/16, 18/16, 10/16, 7/16, etc. These time signatures were removed from the published version as Carter considered them distracting, as indeed they are—the music is much easier to read without them. This continuously changing time signature means that the bar line is determined by the irregular pattern of each phrase. This is almost the opposite of what Schoenberg did in his twelve-tone piano pieces. He wrote atonal music but continuously demanded tonal phrasing, that is, the kind of classical phrasing that would be appropriate for Brahms. (In fact, Schoenberg's piano music should be played with a kind of Brahmsian Viennese phrasing.) But Carter employs a kind of atonal phrasing in a partially tonal work.

The continuous change of meter is typical of much twentieth-century music but is given an entirely new meaning in this piece by the very original use of ostinato. The passage beginning in measure 52 alternates between 14/16 and 12/16 but sounds natural and enormously convincing in the way that it moves. It finally goes off into an entirely different rhythm.

The use of ostinato stems from Stravinsky's neoclassical style in which many of Carter's first pieces were written, but what is different here is the progressively accelerating movement. Stravinsky employed an irregular ostinato, that is, an ostinato which does not repeat itself exactly every time. *The Rite of Spring* is full of these kinds of ostinato which are piled one on top of another and build tremendous tension just by having them repetitiously go on. But they do not progress: they work cumulatively. The only attempt at irregular but progressive ostinato that comes to mind is Bartók's Etude op. 18, no. 3. For two pages Bartók tries it but then settles down into a steady 6/8 because he cannot think what to do with it. Although a very short work, it is in some ways like the opening movement of Carter's Sonata. As far as I know, the technique has not been exploited in another large work. In the passage quoted above, the ostinato figure both accelerates and rises up the scale. The rising is not quite diatonic nor is it chromatic, but very much related to the conception of the sonority of fifths and the attempt to cut into that by the major-minor third relationship that dominates the piece throughout.

There are a great many traditional elements in this Sonata, of course. The sonata form of the first movement has a clear exposition of the first and second themes, a development section, and a recapitulation. The recapitulation is unusual in the way it is marvelously dovetailed with the development: it begins in the middle of the phrase. There is, of course, a classical tradition behind even that: there are a number of cases of Haydn doing it, although the tradition was largely lost in the nineteenth century. The second movement (with its slow section—large ternary form fugue—slow section) is also fairly traditional. There are many other traditional elements in the work including the obvious influence of Stravinsky and Hindemith and even an allusion to Copland's cowboy style in the fugue.

This passage has always amused me, and there must have been a certain amusement on Carter's part: the theme appears four times consecutively, and its rhythmic configuration is entirely and surprisingly different each time. I think every pianist enjoys the wit imposed on an allusion like this.

What I am trying to demonstrate is that while some of the classicism in this work is imposed from without, much of it is reconquered from within. In other words, the outward shape of the piece is a relatively conventional sonata in which there are some very radical musical materials. It is significant that the piece opens not with a theme but with the sonority of the octave Bs out of which all the themes emerge. Deriving themes from the actual sound is a very extraordinary development in the history of music, and one which Carter's subsequent compositions extend in an even more radical way. If I am right about the first movement and much of the second movement as well, even the tonality is not the traditional triadic tonality but is a reinvented tonality. Carter achieves the sense of B major without the tonic-dominant relationships and without much use of a B-major triad. The central feeling of B major stems from the sonority of the piano itself and the harmonics it can produce.

One of the great ambitions of music of our time, particularly of the so-called avant-garde, is to do away with the sense of measured time or clock time—in fact, to do away with the kind of music that you can play with a metronome. Carter gives metronome marks in the Sonata but the metronome is no help when the time signature changes from 10/16 to 14/16. All the metronome marks tell you is how fast to play, but you cannot practice with them, as you can with nineteenth-century music.

This idea of doing away with measured time is an ancient dream of composers and has been spoken about a great deal in this century by Boulez, Cage, and Carter himself.[2] In the nineteenth century Schumann quoted a passage from a novel by a forgotten writer named Wagner (not Richard but Johann Ernst) which suggested that the composer who could overcome the tyranny of the bar line would become the savior of music, make it more like the song of the nightingale who pours forth her melody without having to measure it or chop it into equal eighth notes. In Schumann's review of Liszt's piano arrangement of Berlioz's *Symphonie Fantastique*, he wondered if perhaps Berlioz was to be that savior of music. There are many passages in Berlioz's symphony where the sense of bar line is lost. Even so, the generation of Schumann and Berlioz paradoxically gave the bar line a greater tyranny over music than it had ever had before. As I have implied, doing away with the bar line required also doing away with triadic tonality.

More recently, composers have attempted to eliminate the feeling of measured time through aleatoric music. The danger connected with aleatoric music is obviously that the composer abdicates all control over his piece, and Carter has never been able to agree to this.

Carter begins the movement to overcome the confinements of regular meter with the Piano Sonata. The continually shifting bar line relieves the sense of absolutely strict measurement throughout most of the piece. This is extended in his Cello Sonata, which has the first example that I know of what I shall call polytempo. One senses from the very beginning of the piece that the piano and cello are playing in different tempos and are not just playing cross-rhythms. A cross-rhythm is measured by the coincidence of the beats at the bar line. In Carter's music, the bar lines are only reference points. The places where the beats coincide are not important.

This technique is further extended in the Double Concerto. In the great slow movement, the wind instruments play an expressive and deeply moving chorale in even notes. Over this chorale, in strict tempo, the strings pizzicato, and the piano, harpsichord and percussion staccato; all play a continuously accelerating movement. Of course, it is difficult to see this in the score. The conductor must beat an accelerating tempo against which the wind parts are written to sound as if they are in steady tempo. The result is an extremely peculiar and complicated notation. I have often wondered if it would be a good idea to write out in the wind instruments' parts what they are really supposed to sound like in strict tempo just to calm the players' nerves.

Elliott Carter's music is supposed to be difficult to play. Carter once quoted a remark by a member of the Boston Symphony who said, "The trouble with your music is that it doesn't make sense if you don't play the dynamics." I would go further than that. Until the musicians know why these rhythms are notated the way they are it will be impossible to play the music meaningfully. There is a passage in the introduction of the Double Concerto in which the orchestra is very clearly playing six beats to the measure against which the piano plays a staccato ten to the bar. The bassoon must enter on the second quintuplet of the second beat.

The bassoonist will look at his part and question the purpose of what seems to him a crazy mathematical precision that nobody is going to notice. The reason for this precision is that in this passage some of the instruments in the orchestra play with the piano, but, unlike the piano, sustain each of the notes to make a chord. When the players are aware of this the music becomes more reasonable as well as much easier to play. I know about the bassoonist because he sits next to the piano. When he complained to me, I said, "All you have to do is pick up my second note. We're both playing in five." And he said, "Oh, is that all it is?" From then on he played the note quite happily, and we were always together and there was never any problem about that passage. In other words, the notation made sense.[3]

This is one of the great problems of contemporary music. The bar line in the Double Concerto is largely not heard or felt at all. The conductor indicates beats and measures which do not always coincide with the pulse of the music but which serve as a point of reference to keep the ensemble together. Some beat has to be chosen as a downbeat, but it does not necessarily sound like a downbeat or measure out time in discrete periods.

At this point I would like to return to the difficulty of modern music and say that the difficulty of listening to Carter is an illusory one. It is sometimes said that it is impossible to hear all those notes. Actually, you can hear more of the notes in Carter's music than you can in that of Richard Strauss. What you cannot hear are the bar lines, but then you are not supposed to. (I can remember that Carter, on reading a critic who bewailed the complexity of his scores by citing a measure in which there were seventeen beats, said gently to me, "You know, I don't expect my audiences to sit and count up to seventeen.") The difficulty with Carter stems not from hearing what is there, but more from not hearing what you expect to hear because it is not there. For example, an audience watching a performance of one of Carter's orchestral works sees the conductor give a forceful downbeat with the baton and expects something in the music to correspond to that. Very often there is almost nothing; it just happens to be the easiest way at that point of keeping everybody together. If you expect to hear something (and physically you do so react to the conductor's motion), then you feel that you must be missing something in the music or that everybody must be playing wrong notes or in the wrong time, which they very often are. This is not a problem with the string quartets, which partly for this reason have had less difficulty in winning an audience—or, rather in winning performances. It is, of course, much easier for a string quartet than for a large orchestra to learn new music, and furthermore, a quartet can perform a new work repeatedly and with ever greater understanding. The result for Carter has been that his three string quartets are often performed and with ever greater success.

I would like to finish by suggesting how, in Carter's music, the language is reinvented in the terms of each individual piece. In the Double Concerto the material is gradually introduced in fragments. Tiny bits of sonority come together built from the sound of the dozens of percussion instruments, the timbre of harpsichord, piano, and the two small orchestras. Towards the end of the piece everything falls apart, disintegrating in a reverse action from the opening. Sonority and timbre determine form. In the Piano Concerto, which came some years later, a new way was found to give meaning, significance, and above all, character to a piece which has renounced tonal harmony and tonal rhythm. The solution is achieved through what I would call the periodicity of intervals, and in this way directly from the sonority. The interval of a sixth, for example, has a specific kind of sonority and, in Carter, its own rhythm that brings this out. As Carter uses them in the Piano Concerto, sixths are generally given a rather heavy sound and a slow periodicity, with an almost Brahmsian characteristic. The interval of a second, by contrast, has a much lighter sound and a faster period, and this gives a scherzando quality to the sections where it dominates. In each subsection of the first movement every interval will occur with a certain rhythm and attack of its own. Of course, these passages are not separated in a brutal or simplistic way. Each section has echoes of the other sections within it, and a new section always starts before the present one is over. The result is the entrance of a new rhythm that is not perceptibly commensurable with the first one; and the new intervals come in with an entirely new character, as the light, witty, scherzando seconds gradually take over the heavier, darker quality of the sixths: the work progresses by these changes of sound.

The problem for performers-is how to exploit these changes of character, which means that the tempo relationships must be interpreted relatively strictly. Perhaps we may describe the difference between Carter's music and that of any other contemporary composer in the following way: in Carter's music we have ideals similar to those of all the important avant-garde music of our time (including even the music of John

Cage, which seems to be at the opposite pole from Carter's own), but Carter's music is more ambitious in attempting a genuine control of the most radical effects. The music of Pierre Boulez, another composer of great stature, achieves a sense of nonmeasured time, but in a way that is less demanding. Boulez's music generally demands to be played with a floating beat: the rhythms must be fairly exact on a small-scale, but the music is most often conceived with a floating tempo within which there are continuous ritards and accelerandos. Carter's music demands a small-scale freedom and rubato even within the most complicated works, but the large scale is always held within a tight frame. A sense of nonmeasured time in his work results from a sense of conflict among various concepts of time that are all realized simultaneously. For example, in Carter's String Quartet no. 3 the music is divided into two duos each playing its own set of movements. The overlappings and the coincidences are marvelously thought out, but one is still conscious of the fact that there are two different pieces or at least two different and simultaneous conceptions of tempo, movements, character, and sentiment.

The Concerto for Orchestra carries the conception of the Third Quartet one step further. In this work there are four movements, all of which are played together. At different points one movement will dominate, but the others can still be heard. For example, the distinction between the second and fourth movements is very simple: the second movement starts very fast and gradually slows down while the fourth movement starts with slow fragments and then accelerates. Each of these movements is given to different groups of instruments and each has an entirely different expressive character. The listener can actually hear one movement getting faster and the other getting slower until they reach the same tempo and their paths cross. The different emotional character of the two movements is combined and exploited in the scheme as well.

A final example of what might be called the invention of the musical language itself comes from the last movement of the Piano Concerto. This movement appears to me to be based on the gradual buildup of an enormous string chord of eighty-one notes. The score looks extremely complicated because every member of the string section plays a different note. Carter himself has commented that after you get beyond twenty or thirty notes played together all sense of pitch is lost. What is important for the listener to hear is the way this cluster gets larger and larger, like an invading fog. The wind and brass instruments are given double patterns which are very regular: these strict, sharply attacked phrases have an almost neutral kind of sound. Against this, the piano plays impassioned declamatory phrases in which the sense of pitch is strongly retained and very much opposed to the whole string sound. In other words, the dramatic quality of the piano is in opposition both to the string sonority and to the rhythmic pattern of the wind instruments. The opposition of piano and orchestra is essential to the idea of the concerto, and it has been renewed by Carter in this opposition of gigantic cluster and individualized sound. This section builds up to an enormous climax, against the very soft string chord, as the string cluster remains pianissimo while it continues to grow. The violence is unleashed in the coda and then falls in exhaustion at the end. Once again, it is from the concept of the sonority and the possibilities of sound that the basis of the musical language of the work is achieved.

Each of the compositions I have mentioned seems to take over where the last one left off and investigate new possibilities. This growth makes Carter's works into a larger unity, as he builds on the tradition he himself has created in a way which allows him to retain a hold on the classical tradition. In the earlier Piano Sonata he was able to reconstruct exactly what was necessary for him of that part of tonality which was related to the basic sonority of the piano and to the language of the piece as he conceived it. The later works invent a language based in turn on the former works, but change it radically in each instance. In this sense Elliott Carter's ambitions are larger than those of any other composer of our time and they elucidate the greatness of his achievement.

Editor's Notes

1. This lecture was given before the composition of *Night Fantasies*.
2. See Carter's "Music and the Time Screen" in *Current Thought in Musicology*, ed. John W. Grubbs (Austin: University of Texas Press, 1976).
3. For Carter's explication of this same passage see his "The Orchestral Composer's Point of View" in *The Composer's Point of View: Essays on Twentieth-Century Music by Those Who Wrote It*, ed. Robert Stephan Hines (Norman: University of Oklahoma Press, 1970).

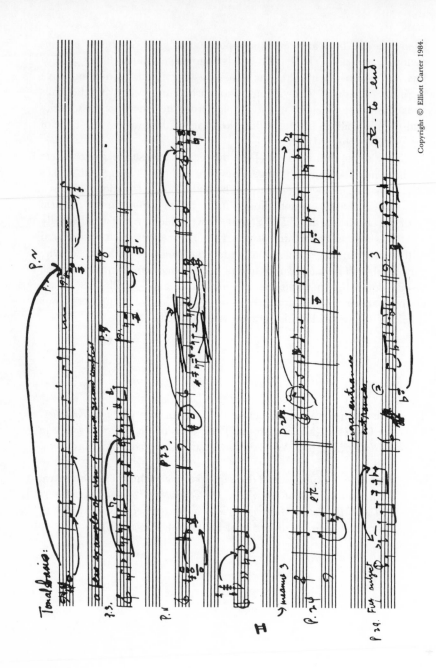

16

Carter's analysis of the tonal basis of his Piano Sonata. Manuscript in the Music Division, Library of Congress.

17

On the verso of Carter's analysis of the tonal basis of his Piano Sonata, the composer has written out the "melodic row" of the fugue episode and then shown how the episode is based on the rhythm of the fugue subject. He has also written out the ways in which the fugue subject has been shortened. Manuscript in the Music Division, Library of Congress.

The first page of the composer's fair copy of his Piano Sonata. Manuscript in the Music Division, Library of Congress.

One Easy Piece

by Charles Rosen

Can a new work of music be played brilliantly by musicians who think that it is impossible to get through it technically with confidence, and also be wildly cheered to the galleries by a public most of whom would claim that it is too complex to understand? So it would seem from the first performance of Elliott Carter's Third Quartet by the Juilliard String Quartet in New York on January 23, 1973. It appears certain that, for all its alleged difficulty, this fascinating work will become a permanent addition to the chamber repertory. Carter's first and second quartets, generally acknowledged as the greatest works in their medium since Bartók, have already achieved this status.

Orchestral works have a harder time making their way. However, at the end of April 1972, Carter's Variations for Orchestra was played four times in one week in New York: three times by the New York Philharmonic and once by the Chicago Symphony. Although this work is a regular part of the Chicago Symphony's repertory (they have played it all over Europe), it was the first performance by the New York Philharmonic.

Variations for Orchestra was written in 1955, and was Carter's only major symphonic work before the Concerto for Orchestra of 1969. That Carter should have had to wait seventeen years for its performance by America's reputedly most distinguished orchestra is typical of the difficult relation between American composer and orchestra today. During these seventeen years—and early enough in them—Carter had been recognized internationally, and considered by many as the finest and most interesting American composer now writing; for most of these seventeen years, in spite of this widespread recognition, the New York Philharmonic had chosen to act as if he did not exist.

The myth of the unrecognized genius is a necessary part of the public aspect of art today. It is important for a radically new work to be understood only little by little and too late: that is the only tangible proof we have of its revolutionary character. There has never, of course, been a truly neglected genius in the history of music—at least not since the time that we have any real data on the lives of composers. Even Schubert, who died so young that appreciation of his stature was only begining to grow, was already well enough known beyond the small world of Viennese music for the young Schumann, when he heard of his death, to have wept uncontrollably all night.

Nor is Carter himself in any way a neglected figure. With the appearance of his First String Quartet in 1949, he almost at once achieved the kind of international fame that would satisfy any ambition. The New York Philharmonic's neglect of his work is therefore an empty ritual, a symbol of the gap that has opened up in our time between performance and composition.

In 1969, the Philharmonic took notice of Carter, but not to play the Variations. It commissioned a new work, to be written especially for the celebration of its centenary. The Concerto for Orchestra, as its title implies, is a work requiring exceptional virtuosity from the players and was immediately accepted as one of Carter's most imaginative achievements. It would, of course, have been much easier to play for an orchestra that was already familiar with Carter's style through the Variations. (It would also have been easier to grasp by a public that was not listening to a work by Carter for the first time—a work, too, of far greater difficulty than the Variations.)

All these barriers to appreciation would no doubt create a reputation for difficulty with any composer. But it is important to note that Carter's distinction has been won neither in spite of this reputation nor because of it. To a great extent—and this is one of the paradoxes of American musical life—it is assumed that because Carter has developed an original style by purely musical procedures and with no recourse to the doctrinaire shenanigans of many of his contemporaries, his music must *therefore* be hard to grasp. To the normal difficulties of playing any new music of any originality is added our expectation that avant-garde art must puzzle, shock, and, above all, resist immediate understanding. Both performer and listener come to a new work by Carter with a conviction of initially insurmountable problems. Our sense of history and the organization of our musical life combine to help us realize these comical fears.

The problem of difficulty in contemporary music is most often wrongly posed. It is generally believed that music is difficult to comprehend either when there is too much going on for the ear to distinguish or when the composer's form—harmonic, melodic, or architectural—is in some mysterious way beyond the grasp of the mind of the listener. Yet both these conditions may be fulfilled and the music still seem lucid and even popular in style.

In the music of Richard Strauss—to take only the most notorious example—not only do a great many of the notes remain totally indistinguishable from an enormous mass of busywork, but the composer was clearly far from caring if they were. "Gentlemen, you are playing all the notes," he is reported to have gasped, appalled, at a rehearsal of *Don Juan* with the Boston Symphony.[1] As for the understanding of form, I remember a group of college students, all music majors, who did not realize that in a sixty-bar piece of Bach I had just played for them, the last twenty bars were the first twenty repeated without alteration. The appreciation of form of the average audience cannot, I think, be rated very high, and yet it has never prevented their enjoyment. Yet those who take in their stride the most abstruse complexities of Beethoven, the subtlest nuances of Mozart, and the most complex effects of Wagner or

Mahler, will stalk angrily out of the hall when presented with, say, the enchanting simplicities of Alban Berg's post-card lieder.

It is paradoxically not what is actually to be heard that makes music difficult, but what cannot be heard because it is not there. It is the lack of something which the listener expects to hear but which is refused him that makes his blood boil, that brings the aged Philharmonic subscriber to the verge of apoplexy.[2] Every original work represents an omission, even a deliberate erasure of what was previously indispensable to art, as well as a new ordering and new elements. The real irritant for the listener is that what he has so far considered as essential to a work of music he now cannot perceive. The composer has left it out. The appreciation of a new style is as much an effort of renunciation as of acceptance.[3]

To see what Carter refuses to allow the listener is a preliminary necessity to a comprehension of his art; in the end it will be the same as seeing what he has brought to music. What an original composer "leaves out," however, is rarely what the public, or the average musician for that matter, thinks. We have only to remember the reproaches that there was no melody in Wagner, no form in Beethoven, no coherence to Schumann, or that the music of Mozart could appeal only to the head and not to the heart.

To show something of the gradual process of understanding a new composer's thought, I can mention my own experience with Carter's most brilliantly attractive and apparently most complex work, the Double Concerto for the piano, harpsichord, and two small chamber orchestras. This is a work which has had, happily, a considerable history of performance. At its premiere (in which I played) it was felt that future performances would be rare. The requirement of four virtuoso percussion players, each playing more than ten instruments, was alone sufficiently dismaying. Yet it has been recorded three times and given hundreds of performances by many different groups. I have played in more than a third of the performances and in both recordings, so that for once I have some personal knowledge of the unfolding hisory of our understanding of a work of music. The original difficulties of performance—and of hearing—transformed themselves, becoming at once easier to deal with and more problematical, both more traditional and tied to a new vision of the art of music.

In the summer of 1961, I received the last pages of the piano part of the Double Concerto in Paris a few days before flying to New York for the first rehearsal. It is not only eighteenth-century musicians, waiting for Mozart to blot the wet ink on the score, who have had to learn a new work at the last minute. (Recently for Boulez's *Eclat-Multiples* the copyists were working until the day before the first performance.) The final section or coda of the Double Concerto contained the most complicated rhythmic passage I had ever been asked to play, a few measures of moderately fast septuplets against triplets—that is, while the right hand plays seven even notes to each beat, the left hand plays three. The real complication comes from the division of the septuplets into groups of four by a melody (marked *singing and expressive*) whose line consisted of every fourth note. The most complicated cross-rhythm I had seen before this was the famous eight against nine in Brahms's Variations on a Theme by Paganini. The Carter seven against three was more difficult because of the internal subdivision of the sevens and, paradoxically, because of the slightly slower beat—so that the irregularities were easier to hear. (As we shall see, this passage will turn out to be not a true cross-rhythm at all, but something quite different.)

I had not yet succeeded in persuading my left hand to ignore what my right hand was doing when I had to leave for New York and one of New York's late-summer heat waves. Rehearsals took place during a ten-day period in which the weather frustrated a sane and cool approach to a difficult new work. The luxury of ten days of rehearsal was due to the generosity of Paul Fromm, who commissioned the work and allowed the composer his choice of performers. The small chamber orchestra was made up of the best of New York's free-lance players with a considerable awareness of contemporary style. The conductor was the young Swiss, Gustave Meier; the harpsichordist, the older and more experienced Ralph Kirkpatrick. Kirkpatrick's experience, however, was almost entirely in eighteenth-century music, his style of playing was heavily dependent on the kind of freedom (or rubato) most appropriate for Baroque music. This did not prevent him from giving an impressive account of the work, the solo cadenza in particular; one of the graces of his performance was indeed a tension between an older style of playing and a newer style of writing.[4]

But Kirkpatrick had recently undergone an eye operation which exacerbated the most ticklish problem of the Double Concerto: the seating arrangement. Each of the two solo instruments is placed in front of its own small orchestra of six men: two strings, two winds, and two brass. The separation between the two orchestras (and, therefore, the two soloists) should be both visually and audibly evident. Spread out over a half circle behind the two orchestras are four percussion players, each with a formidable array of about a dozen instruments to cope with. The harpsichordist, in front of his orchestra, and two percussion players are on the left of the stage as the audience sees them; the pianist and his ensemble to the right. The problem is to place the conductor so that he can see and be seen by both soloists and both orchestras. There are various solutions possible, but the wide separation of the two chamber orchestras and the danger that the raised lids of the two solo keyboards might hide the conductor from part of the orchestra created unexpected difficulties.

This new technical obstacle arose from a new and even revolutionary conception of the use of space in performance. Contrast of two or more groups, echo effects, and other static devices are common enough, and have been since the sixteenth century when the Venetians decided to exploit the immensity of the interior of St. Mark's. In Carter's Double Concerto, however, the choirs are not merely set off against each other, but the music describes arabesques in space as rhythms are passed from one musician to another. The simplest example of this is a roll on the cymbals that goes from right to left as each one of the percussionists takes it up, overlapping with the previous one.

The most elaborate use of the spatial arabesque is in the slow movement, where the winds and brass intone a soft chorale-like texture in strict time and—imposed like a grid over this—a continuously and uniformly accelerating (and, later, decelerating) rhythm is played with great delicacy by piano, harpsichord, and percussion staccato and strings pizzicato, each instrument playing only one or two notes as the steadily changing rhythm passes around the orchestra. It is a beautiful conception, but difficult to notate: everybody's part must be written to refer to the conductor's beat, the conductor must direct the continuously accelerating instruments, and when an absolutely simple and even rhythm is written to conform to a continuously changing beat, it comes out looking very queer indeed.

Some of the members of the orchestra in many of the performances had such difficulty trying to place their notes relative to a uniformly changing beat that they never realized that their own parts are actually played in strict time. Their difficulties, indeed, were aggravated by the fact that when the acceleration has proceeded to a certain point, the conductor's beat has become so fast that for purely physical reasons he must shift to beating only the longer note values—without, however, interrupting the acceleration. At these moments the beat becomes three times as slow, and the notation three times as fast, and it is difficult for most musicians to make the shift imperceptible to the audience.

At the first rehearsal, the passage in the coda that had so frightened me in Paris (three against seven, with the sevens accented in groups of four) became far more terrifying when I at last saw the full score. The piano and its small orchestra have their parts notated in three beats to the measure, the rhythm of septuplets in the right hand therefore coming out to twenty-one notes against the nine (three triplets) per measure in the left; but the harpsichord and its orchestra have their music written in two beats per measure, the harpsichord playing five notes per beat in the right hand against four in the left, or ten against eight per measure—with the quintuplets accented every third note, the quadruplets every fifth, *so that the accents of all four lines in piano and harpsichord never coincide.*[5] The already complex cross-rhythms of twenty-one against ten against nine against eight were made infinitely more difficult by the subdivisions of phrase and accent.

It was some time afterward that I began to realize slowly and painfully (how slowly I am ashamed to confess) that these were not cross-rhythms at all, at least not as they had always been understood so far in music. Brahms's eight against nine in the Variations on a Theme by Paganini is a true cross-rhythm because the beginning of each group of eight and nine—their moment of coincidence—is clearly marked. There is, in short, a central beat in Brahms which occurs every eight (or, in the left hand, every nine) notes, and which provides a frame. We hear a larger, slower rhythm within which the cross-rhythms are to be understood.

What Carter has done is to remove the central beat—except for purposes of pure notation. No central beat can be heard: the rhythms

26

therefore do not cross, but proceed independently. They are, in fact, cross-tempi or cross-speeds, if you like. The occasional coincidence of accent in two parts no longer refers to the existence of a slower and all-governing beat, but to periodic movements which have momentarily come together and are about to spread apart once again. There *is* a central rhythmic frame of reference in the Double Concerto but it is no longer a static and immovable principal beat; the frame is the system by which one tempo is transformed into another in the course of the piece. The central rhythmic conception cannot be heard as completely revealed at any one moment of the work, but is a function of the work as a whole.

In other words, those complicated-looking septuplets divided into groups of four in the right hand of the piano part were not septuplets at all, and not in the least complicated: they were simple groups of four. They coincide with the left hand rhythm every seven notes, but the moments of coincidence are not supreme, have no privilege. But they are what the conductor must beat to keep the ensemble together.

Music is "difficult," as I said above, when we are listening for something which is not there. It is not the multiplicity of rhythm in this passage that creates the initial impression of obscurity. The four different superimposed tempi are clearly audible: we can all hear, in a beautifully transparent texture with ravishing tone color, four lines moving at four different rates of speed. Four different lines are, suprising as that may seem, very easy to perceive when clearly different in rhythm, and have always been easy in music from Bach to the present; they merely demand a carefully nuanced and sensitive performance.

But when we ask—as we do after our experience of traditional music— "what in the *basic* rhythm?" we receive no answer from Carter where we have always had one from Bach. Debussy's writing, for example, is always exquisitely balanced, rich, and harmonious, but when his public asked, "What is the key?" "What is the central chord?" and received no answer, the music seemed an intolerable succession of dissonances. Critics have sometimes complained of Carter that many of his notes cannot be heard, where in fact everything in his work is as easy to hear, as transparent as the scores of Mahler, Berg, Ives, or Tchaikovsky. Paradoxically the Double Concerto appears most difficult to musicians who are trying to follow the score. The bar lines traditionally mark a regular strong beat: in Carter they are often a purely visual aid to the ensemble with only occasionally a genuine significance for the ear.[6]

The reliance of the public upon the conductor's movements for the sense of what they are hearing leads to an analogous misunderstanding. For many people the gestures of the conductor are a guide: they interpret the piece, clarify its rhythm, indicate the climaxes, tell them what to feel. In the Double Concerto the conductor's beat does not indicate a central rhythm, but only one of two or more equally important lines, and the public is often puzzled to hear nothing fundamental that corresponds to the most vigorous gestures. They conclude that something has gone wrong with the ensemble—and matters are not helped by the fact that occasionally something has.

Musicians take almost as long as—and sometimes longer than—the public to accept and understand something new in music. They are as dependent as the audience upon the gestures of the conductor for a feeling of security. But the conductor's beat largely must correspond to the notation. The bar line is the traditional place for the conductor's down beat, and it generally means the strong beat, the mark of the dominating central pulse which often disappears from Carter's music.

At one point, indeed, in the Double Concerto, traditional notation is stretched beyond its limits and even abandoned, if only briefly. The climax of the slow movement is a brilliant and enchanting one: the piano and the harpsichord have been softly accompanying long melodies in the wind instruments; then, as the harpsichord and both orchestras begin to slow down in an immensely long ritard, the piano begins gradually to accelerate more and more until its notes end in a soft, resonant blur. It is a beautifully poetic effect; and an extraordinarily simple and direct one. A gradual acceleration against a gradual deceleration, however, would require for its exact notation the solution of a differential equation of the second degree. The points of coincidence between piano and orchestra are therefore only approximately notated in the score. In playing this passage, I have always found it best not to look at the conductor at all and just pray that it will come out right. It generally does, as the extreme speed of the repeated notes at the end demanded by Carter represent the technical limits of the instrument as well as of the performer.

The mood of the first performance was one close to panic. In particular the last section of the piece, with one orchestra's part notated in 6/8, the other in 3/4, caused special anxiety. "I feel more like a traffic cop than a conductor," said Gustave Meier, trying to balance the sonority of one orchestra against another. Would we get through the piece without breaking down? We made it to the end. I had no clear idea how the performance went, but it turned out to be an enormous success with the public and, the next day, the critics.

The poetic content of the Double Concerto and its dramatic conception imposed themselves at once. The fragments of the introduction that seem to grow together in a continuous organic movement, the end of the slow central section in which the extreme slowing down of the orchestra suddenly becomes identical in its total suspension of movement with the extreme speeding up of the piano carried so far that no increase of motion is audible (like two opposed infinites that meet), the scherzo dramatically broken twice by the violent cadenzas of the piano, and the fierce coda that superimposes all the rhythms of the work in one great sonority and then falls to pieces "and in a flash expires" (like the end of Pope's *Dunciad,* as Carter himself has remarked)—all this was immediately obvious in spite of so much about the music that was not yet clear to the musicians or to the public.

Stravinsky, indeed, spoke of the Double Concerto as the first American masterpiece. What was most evidently masterly, most easily accessible to the general public, was the rich play of sound, not only in contrast and blending of sonority, but in a dynamic conception of one kind of sonority moving into another—piano staccato, violin pizzicato, and bongo drums clearly taking over the successive notes of a single rhythmic phrase, for example. Virtuosity, too, is still a direct and legitimate way to the public heart, and the virtuoso passages in the Double Concerto for the harpsichordist, the pianist, and four percussion players are spectacular. So difficult, in fact, are the percussion parts that these players generally tend to swamp the others—less from an inability to damp their instruments than from an attempt to give themselves confidence by more vigorous and hearty thumps.

No matter what the performance is like, the work is almost player-proof, always a success. The only exception occurred the following year in London when it was directed by the greatest conductor to have done the piece to this day, Hans Rosbaud. The work had already been played in London a few months previously under Jacques-Louis Monod, one of the finest and most intelligent young conductors. His performance was exciting, with great vitality, but half the rehearsals were devoted to changing the seating arrangements of the orchestra and soloists. In one of these periodic redistributions, I bumped my head on a pendant microphone and had three stitches sewn in my scalp.

Rosbaud, a courteous gentle man, beloved by orchestral musicians, had devoted a great part of his life to contemporary music. When he directed the Double Concerto at a festival of the International Society for Contemporary Music in London, he was a dying man, the cancer that was to kill him six months later already far advanced. The program, as at most such international occasions when each country must be represented, was far too long. On this one evening there were major works from England, France, Italy, and Poland, as well as the Double Concerto.

Rosbaud was fascinated with the Double Concerto but had not realized its difficulties when studying it (if indeed, he had been able to study it at all). He confided to me that it was the only work on the program he liked, along with a beautiful song cycle by Thaddeus Baird. Accordingly, he rehearsed the Double Concerto and little else, as the Baird songs were much easier. Rehearsals took place in an atmosphere heavy with resentment, smoldering with tension, as other composers and soloists waited around for their scheduled turn, only to be told that Rosbaud wished to continue rehearsing Carter's work.

It was a measure of the greatness of Rosbaud's character as well as a poor omen for the performance that, as we were about to step onto the stage, he turned to me and said, "Tell me, where were those places I was beating wrong this morning?" The performance did not break down, but it was a dead one, drained of all vitality; in part this was due to one of the lead players then in the BBC symphony, who hated contemporary music and was doing his discreet best to sabotage the festival. Carter, who was there, was ashen afterward. It is a terrible thing for a composer to hear one of his works played with most of the right notes and no musical life.

At all other times, the Double Concerto seems to have created excitement against whatever odds. There have been beautifully controlled, relaxed, convincing performances by Gunther Schuller. There have, of course, been many performances that I have neither played in nor heard. A measure of the progress of our understanding of the work was a performance in New York under Dennis Russel Davies at Tully Hall. When the work was first played in 1961, there were ten full days of rehearsal. In 1972, for a completely relaxed execution, less than half that time was necessary. The New York musicians were beginning to learn how to deal with the piece.

It was in these performances that certain aspects of the music began to be clear. As we all gradually shed our fears of getting lost, of the performance breaking down, as we stopped accenting the down beat in a desperate effort to keep together, and started phrasing the music as it asked to be phrased, making the delicate nuances that Carter had written, we began to hear things we had never suspected in the work. The enchanting play of intervals, each with its own periodic rhythm, moving in and out of phase with each other, suddenly became clear.

We realized that the absence of one dominant pulse did not mean a loss of control, but that it made possible a new and powerfully expressive set of relations between the apparently independent voices. In fact, Carter's rhythmic innovations—which are now famous—can be seen as affecting all the other elements of music, and even as radically altering our conception of the nature of music itself. Carter's recent works—the new quartet in particular—can no longer be heard as purely linear, narrative progressions in time, but as the intersection of opposed forces in a kaleidoscopic pattern.

Paradoxically, the most satisfying performance of the Double Concerto I have played in took place with students at the New England Conservatory in Boston, directed with love and understanding by Frederik Prausnitz. Students have a great advantage over full professionals for a work of this kind: they do not have to be paid for rehearsals, and they are usually eager to take the music home and really work on it. The Double Concerto, too, needs only one violin, one cello, one oboe, etc., and any important conservatory can generally provide one first-rate player on every instrument. The New England Conservatory has a uniquely deep stage, and the problems of the seating arrangement solved themselves at once with an incomparable gain for the spatial conception of the work.

The history of the Double Concerto is one of a gradual but irregular progress of understanding, perception, and sympathy. When the work first appeared, there were hardly any performers who did not, at least secretly, regret the absence of the central pulse that made ensemble playing so much easier, just as those who saw the first cubist pictures must necessarily have felt—along with a liberated excitement—a curious anxiety at the loss of the central point of view destroyed by cubist fragmentation. A multiplicity of vision has become central to the artistic imagination of the twentieth century. Carter's is the richest and most coherent realization of this multiplicity in the music of our time. The simplicity and directness of his achievement, however, its permanence and its solidity, are only beginning to be felt.

Notes

1. Perhaps even more revealing was his ironic reproach to Toscanini: "In my music there are good and bad notes; when I conduct it, I can hear only the good ones, but when you conduct it, I can hear all the notes."

2. We should not underestimate the physical effects of incomprehension. I recall that when, at the age of seventeen, I first heard the Bartók String Quartet no. 5, it made me physically sick.

3. And not only in music. I see from Leo Steinberg's splendid collection of essays *Other Criteria* (Oxford, 1972) that back in 1962 he made a similar point about modern painting.

4. In most of the recent performances, Paul Jacobs has been the elegant and brilliant harpsichordist.

5. The complexity here is exceptional, as the coda sums up the work. The following table may make the system of notation clearer:

Piano right hand: $3 \times 7 = 21$
   (accented groups of four)
Harpsichord right hand: $2 \times 5 = 10$
   (accented groups of three)
Piano left hand: $3 \times 3 = 9$
   (accented groups of seven)
Harpsichord left hand: $2 \times 4 = 8$
   (accented groups of five)

The tempo is moderate, the dynamics very soft, all rhythms exactly even, and the texture transparent. (The accented notes are made by allowing them to continue to sound during the unaccented ones.)

6. It should be remembered that the score is a late Renaissance invention. The complicated polyphonic music of the fourteenth and fifteenth centuries was sung and played without a score, and without bar lines.

An Interview with Elliott Carter

Charles Rosen

To most people, one of the most striking things about your music is the way it seems to come out of the nature of the instruments for which it is written. Would you tell us to what extent this has played a role in your conception of the pieces and when you think this began to be the case?

Elliott Carter

I think it began rather early. I wrote a great deal of choral music in the thirties, and naturally when you write choral music you really have to think about the medium because you are not going to write piano music for a chorus to sing. In any case, I was very concerned with giving singers the kind of lines they were accustomed to and which would express the various feelings that I wanted to present by using the human voice. It was after this experience that I began, bit by bit, to take up the idea of having the music in instrumental works appear to be created directly out of the instrument. The Piano Sonata was a work in which I tried very hard to deal with the sound of the contemporary modern piano—that is, the large concert grand with eighty-eight keys—its sonority and its varied possibilities of touch and pedalling, and even of overtones. I was very much concerned with making the piano the center and having the music come out of that. Now what this involves is something rather interesting. The music has to sound as if it needed the piano to say what it had to say. So that once I decide what instrument I am going to write for, then I cast around and try to find the kind of music suitable for this particular instrument which will make it—even if it is a harpsichord—appear in all its various guises and be eloquent. I was very concerned (from the Piano Sonata on, which was written in 1945) in every case to find not only the voice of the instrument but the expression of the instrument as well.

CR

What is striking about the Piano Sonata, which makes it different from your earlier work, is that it not only exploits the instrument and makes it eloquent but that the actual language of the music seems to come from the instrument. The Sonata is a tonal piece, but it does not use strictly classical tonality. Certain combinations of notes on the piano have greater resonance than others, and you make that the basis of your harmony; a great deal of the rhythm, in fact, comes from that, too. Does that seem to you to be the case?

EC

Oh, yes. Actually this did really start with the Piano Sonata in 1945. Before that I had written—outside of choral music—what you might call works conceived as music that had to be instrumented. There was a prior thought about the music but not about the instrument itself that was going to play it. By the time I composed the Piano Sonata I was really trying to achieve individualization of the instrument, and actually it was not long before I began to feel that this was such an interesting idea—that I could create conflicts between two kinds of instruments with different kinds of expression and ways of being played. From that time on my works played various characters off against each other, and the form of the works derived from this interplay between different instruments: sometimes two instruments, and in the case of large orchestral works, like the Concerto for Orchestra, the entire orchestra. In this piece I was trying to individualize all the parts as if they formed a large crowd of different people.

CR

What has always fascinated me in the oppositions you create is that very often these oppositions are between instruments which are in some cases very similar, like the piano and the harpsichord, so that the opposition is restricted to certain aspects of the playing; then there is always an absolutely fascinating place in each piece where the two begin to blend.

EC

Well, opposition is not exactly the word! In the end, it is hard not to say that this all became anthropomorphic, and that I was also thinking of the players as performers. In a sense I was individualizing not merely the instrument but also the player of the instrument, who became, to a certain extent, a character in the work. In the Cello Sonata, for example, there were two different kinds of characters, the cello and the piano—imaginary characters, so to speak—that maintained different roles and had different ways of looking at the musical field. And in the Double Concerto I was concerned with the different sensitivities of the piano and the harpsichord—obviously they are both keyboard instruments—but the human touch was the interesting thing about this. Now they *do* blend; to write a piece with a continual opposition between the instruments would strain my imagination more than I would care for.

CR

There is an extraordinary place in the Double Concerto, where the opposition is almost removed and then returns, perhaps the most fascinating point of the piece, at the end of the slow movement. The piano and the harpsichord are both playing more or less exactly the same musical line, except that the harpsichord plays sixteen notes to a measure, and the piano plays eighteen notes to a measure.

EC

Don't remind me of that!

CR

The two are just slightly out of phase (the melody notes can be heard clearly because each instrument, playing pianissimo, sustains just those notes), and right after that the opposition is reestablished because the harpsichord and the orchestra gradually get very slow, almost unbearably slow, while the piano becomes so fast that it reaches a kind of point of infinity, a blur or a tremolo just vibrating on one chord.

EC

Actually, that passage interested me a good deal because it is only a moment, or a small section, of a very much longer passage. The drums that are associated with the piano start beating in very slow rhythm and the music gradually speeds up; the piano bursts in and it continues the speeding-up of the drum; the harpsichord starts very rapidly, and then its part peters out. There is an intersection, which is the point you were describing, in which they more or less stabilize for a bit and then they separate: they start apart, then join together, and finally go apart. One of the first times that I was conscious of this dichotomy between two instruments was in the Cello Sonata I wrote in 1948. I started the work without thinking about this, and the more I wrote it, the more it worried me that the sound of the piano was so different from that of the cello. You strike a note on the piano and it fades out, but a cellist can either fade out or grow strong, and make many kinds of attacks that a pianist is not able to do. As I went on writing the piece, this became more and more interesting. So I decided to frame the whole thought of the piece with this idea: the piano being strict and mainly percussive and the cello songful and romantic. And so, after having written three of the movements—the second, third and fourth—I wrote the first movement, which epitomizes this particular aspect and establishes the separate character of these two instruments: the piano playing a kind of clock time and the cello a kind of psychological time.

The Double Concerto was conceived with the idea of surrounding the piano and the harpsichord with instruments that amplified certain aspects of each of them—the piano with membrane percussion (like drums) and the harpsichord with tinkling and wooden instruments that suggested the various kinds of attacks that the harpsichord has. The point was to have two small orchestras that were distinct and different in sound, just as the piano and harpsichord were, but within which were also planted examples of the other type so that we could have, for example, a sweep round the entire vista from one percussion player after another playing a cymbal roll. Not only was I concerned with the opposition but also with having a world in which everything would be joined together. And this became a primary concern in all of my music from that time on. The Double Concerto has a certain chordal system which isolates the piano from the harpsichord, but at the same time when the two instruments are sounded together they produce another chord, a chord that runs through the whole work and gives it a certain general sound. And in works after that I began to explore all kinds of harmonic possibilities—combinations of intervals that would both isolate elements and combine them to make a general chord, like a tonic, that would unify the piece. I began to realize, as many people did after the war when the Darmstadt school started and aleatoric music had become fashionable, that the idea of having uncoordinated, separate things destroyed all sense of drama. From my point of view it is not dramatic to have two things going on simultaneously that are not connected in some way, not necessarily immediately intelligible but at least partially intelligible. We are so continually confronted in our lives with things that do not go together, that I feel music should somehow give the impression that things do go together, no matter how remotely they are connected.

CR

That is why the moments of the blending of oppositions that one finds in your works seem so fascinating. What is also striking, and I do not think it has been sufficiently understood, is that the complexities of rhythm in your music are not arbitrarily imposed but arise from the sonority; and they are also a way of dramatizing the emotional complexity. Both harmony and rhythm exploit the conflicts between various instruments and then draw them together in a kind of common sound, when two rhythmic or harmonic systems meet. Sometimes, indeed, there are more than two systems, as in the Piano Concerto.

EC

Well, after I have worked a good deal on a piece, an idea that coordinates everything becomes an important matter; the random is not something that I am interested in expressing. The exploitation of musical relationships more remote than those that were worked out in the past is what is really interesting—that is, more remote relationships of harmony, of instrumental sound, and of ensemble playing. As you say, a lot of the combinations of rhythm are not imposed in my music; they arise partly from the fact that I do not want to give the impression of a simultaneous motion in which everybody's part is coordinated like a goose step. I do not want to write the kind of music that just marches on and marches off. I want it to seem like a crowd of people, or like waves on the sea—all things that signify a much more fluid and, to me, more human way of living.

CR

I was struck by what you said about the beginning of the Cello Sonata (which represents another breakthrough in your work, like the Piano Sonata). You remarked that the two instruments exist in different kinds of time; the piano in clock time, measuring off the bars rather strictly because of its percussive quality, and the cello in a much more eloquent or psychological time. That is what I meant by saying that these oppositions of rhythm in your work come partly from the emotional complexity of the harmony—at least I have noticed that in a sort of unsystematic way while playing your music. For example, in the Piano Concerto the sixths have a rather slow period because they are heavy sound, while the seconds come much faster because they are lighter. So the rhythm in your work exploits the quality of sounds—not only of the instruments but of the intervals as well—and therefore contributes to the harmony.

EC
In the Piano Concerto each one of the eleven intervals was assigned—after a good deal of experimentation, let me say!—a certain speed area, and, as you say, sixths were comparatively slow. But then I also made passages in which there were combinations of sixths and seconds, so that there would be a fast counterpoint, or a combination of sixths and fourths, sometimes even a counterpoint of three different kinds of intervals, so that I was able to make all types of textures.

CR
And of course there are not just strict rhythmic textures in which every interval is ruthlessly assigned a speed, but also rubato movements, free movements in which the piano accelerates, retards, and plays strictly at the same time.

EC
I felt that the piano was like Montaigne—a man with many various changes of character and feeling (*l'homme ondoyant et divers*).

CR
For a long time you were more famous for the string quartets than for anything else, possibly because there were so many groups who had your quartets in their repertoire and played them frequently, so that one heard them more often than any of your other works.

EC
Of course the string quartet is a very different medium from the double concerto because, in the end, the four strings do sound a great deal alike and merely cover different registers. Therefore I felt it was important to diversify the characters of the instruments, of what these four rather similar-sounding instruments would play. As a result the string quartets had more exaggerated oppositions than the Double Concerto. Actually my Second Quartet was written in the middle of the Double Concerto. While I was writing the Double Concerto, I stopped and wrote the Second Quartet and then went back to the Concerto, so they have many features

in common. The First Quartet was really the first extended effort I made in dealing with what you might call polyrhythmic textures, building a work that had a continuous stream of changes of tempi all superimposed on each other from beginning to end. And that work seemed to be so novel in its time that it did get played a lot by the Juilliard Quartet and many other groups, in spite of its forty-five-minute length and extreme difficulty. In the First Quartet I tried not only to have these streams of very different speeds going on together in many different ways, but also to isolate different themes having different speeds; and there are many combinations of contrasting musical character. But I did not think of giving each one of the four instruments a separate character until the Second Quartet.

CR

That work even innovates with regard to the placement of the performers.

EC

I wanted them to sit on the four corners of the stage, but it turned out that almost every time a quartet tried it they could not do it because the acoustics of the hall made it impossible to hear each other play and so they could not be sure if they were playing together or not. And that worried them and then worried me too, I must say.

CR

You did want them separated more than the traditional seating allows.

EC

They generally get about four or five inches farther apart than is normal, and some get a little bit farther still. I have been toying with the idea of having them all feed the information into some sort of telephonic system so they could sit very far apart and play. My old teacher Walter Piston said "You know, if I were you, I'd put each one of the instruments in a different room and shut the doors!"

CR

The Second Quartet also innovates with regard to the structure of the movements. In order to make the isolation of the instruments more dramatic, each instrument plays the leading role in a different movement. I have always been most fascinated by the movement in which the viola takes the lead.

EC

That is the slow movement. The viola is a rather sobbing instrument in this piece, pathetic and sorry for itself throughout. At times the rest of the quartet sympathize and at other times they think it is ridiculous. So, of the two main movements the viola plays, there is one in which the rest of them play something very different—fast and rather funny little things, while the viola is playing slowly—and another rather long slow movement that the viola leads, in which they all join, in some cases exaggerating what the viola does and in other cases minimizing it.

CR

The seating for the Third Quartet is also innovative, but that too relates just as directly, in fact, even more strikingly, to the form of the piece.

EC

I made the Third Quartet into two duos, one for violin and viola and one for violin and cello. And these are actually two separate sets of pieces from beginning to end. Each duo has a different number of movements. Now, this means that you hear part of the slow movement of one duo against the fast movement of another, but you also hear combinations of tempo and texture much more closely shaded together. What may be interesting about the form is that none of the material ever repeats literally, and this is characteristic of many of my pieces ever since the First Quartet. They never actually repeat the same theme, but they are always improvizing on a basic piece of material that holds together all the various things that are being played. There will sometimes be repetitions of certain speeds and textures that dominate different sections—and the character of these sections (sudden changes from loud to soft, for example) may reappear—but the form is not a form in which there is literal repetition, only a constant repetition of a general principle. This goes right back to my early piece, the Eight Etudes and a Fantasy, in which I attempted to find the elements of musical thought, to discover basically what it is to make musical statements. I wrote a piece on one note, in which the form contrasts various kinds of attacks and various kinds of loudness and softness. Another one of the etudes is entirely built on a minor second: all the instruments play this interval in succession in different transpositions, and this makes up all the material, which is constantly changing throughout the work while the basic building stones remain constant. I have pursued this principle since that 1949 period. Until now my music is almost always without any kind of repetition at all. Maybe you can find one chord that is the same from beginning to end, but the main thing is the sense of constant growth and change.

CR

What is interesting about this principle of nonrepetition (a principle that you have in common with a few other contemporary composers) is that in your music you *do* get the effect of return without literal repetition. It has struck me in playing the *Night Fantasies,* for example, that there are whole passages that seem to return although never literally—textures, sounds, and emotional characters throughout the work give the effect of return. This makes for a new concept of form.

EC

I am also very concerned with how you lead into something that sounds like what you have heard before, and am always concerned with the context of things. Not only, as we were saying, am I concerned with the context of one duo playing against another, as in the Third Quartet (so that each duo gets its meaning or feeling being played against a movement of different characters, and each time something comes back it is contrasted with another part of the quartet and is given a new flavor), but also with the contexts of a return or of a new idea. Sometimes the new section or the return appears very abruptly in the *Night Fantasies,* but generally not; even when there is an abrupt change of texture and sound, usually it is made up of the same notes you have been hearing for the last three measures.

CR

It is like what a tape engineer would call "pre-echo": in the middle of one kind of sound, you suddenly get something which will then turn out to be the basis of the next section. But does this idea of form change when you are dealing with a text, as you have been so often in the last few years in a number of song cycles written for various combinations of instruments and voice?

EC

Well, of course, yes it does, but by the time I came to writing song cycles, which I think I did first in 1976—

CR

On poems of Elizabeth Bishop.

EC

A Mirror on Which to Dwell, yes. By that time I felt I had a very large repertory of ways of dealing with pieces of music. So that all the songs in that cycle summon up musical expression—what we have been talking about in another way. I hope the music is an analogue of the text. There was a poem about breathing, for instance. I made an accompaniment which sounded like one kind of breathing, a very slow rhythm that faded in and out, and juxtaposed against it a rather hysterical kind of breathing for the singer.

CR

Everybody has always been struck by the fact that in the song "The Sandpiper" the oboe really sounds like a bird. It does not, however, sound like the *sound* that a bird makes; it sounds like the way a bird walks or struts.

EC

Well, the sandpiper is the student of Blake who is seeing the world in a grain of sand, and the sandpiper is totally oblivious to the waves and the dangers of the sea. So he is continually moving around, always at the same speed, while all the rest of the song is always changing in speed as the poet considers various aspects of the total scene. I picked out the sandpiper and gave him his fast little notes—sometimes high shrieks.

CR

The literary inspiration of the song cycles was not exactly new for you—at least the program notes that you have written sometimes claim a kind of nonmusical inspiration for some of the purely instrumental works: for example, the Symphony for Three Orchestras. Or is that the Symphony *of* Three Orchestras?

EC

Of Three Orchestras. Yes. The sounding together of three orchestras was the way I thought of it.

CR

Would you discuss the extent to which this is true?

EC

Well, about the program, or the nonliterary, nonmusical aspect of the orchestral works and also of the Double Concerto: it is rather hard for me to say that they were really based on a poem or on an extramusical idea. What actually happened was that there was an initial musical idea in the three cases mentioned—the Piano Concerto is a fourth example. In the Symphony of Three Orchestras, I wanted to write a piece in which there was a constant very gradual downward motion from a very high register to the very lowest register of the orchestra throughout the piece. I also wanted to have many planes of sound mixing together as I did in the Third String Quartet. The Symphony of Three Orchestras is very much like the Third String Quartet, but instead of having two duos, I had three orchestras and I wanted them to mix together and then separate out. As a result, while thinking about this, I began to think about something else I had always wanted to do, and that is make a work that was based on a poem of Hart Crane's called ''The Bridge'' which I had read when I was in college. And then I thought maybe this would be the time to start doing it, so I read ''The Bridge,'' but I decided I did not really think I could write a piece on it: it was much too confused although it had very many beautiful moments. But I began to see that one could take elements out of Hart Crane's poetry that would suggest the total idea of the movement from high to low registers and the blurring of various kinds of characters together; and so, this poetry became a kind of basis for the music. The Symphony of Three Orchestras starts with a vision of New York harbor and a gull flying above it and ends with the suicide of Hart Crane himself: but that is the way I saw it *after* I had the conception of the music.

CR

I have played the Piano Concerto twice, but I never knew there was an extramusical program.

EC

Well, not in any literary sense. I started by thinking about writing a piano concerto in which there would be a very strong opposition between the pianist and the orchestra, with their somehow being initially close together and then the piano gradually diverging from the orchestra over the whole work. I received a grant to go and live in Berlin, where the opposition between the individual and the crowd had had its violent expression in a previous time, in Hitler's time. I felt I was living right in the middle of my own Piano Concerto when I was writing it, and it somehow reflected this strange atmosphere of 1964, of destroyed buildings and the terrible stories that we had heard. There was also the fact that in the end there were people, kindly people, who made it all work again, so that the piece ends with the piano making a quiet final statement which is a solution.

CR

Then, if I understand it correctly, the literary analogue, or the literary inspiration, is in fact not primary but secondary. There is a literary analogue for the musical idea that you find in your reading; it helps you continue, acts as a catalyst, and then you end up going back to the music alone. I know you told me that in one of the pieces you got bored with the literary inspiration itself and just forgot all about it on the way.

EC

That is true. That was the Concerto for Orchestra, where I dealt again with the idea of treating the orchestra as a crowd of individuals. I was attempting to write a piece in which there would be a continually shifting focus on all the members of the orchestra at one time or another. Then someone told me about St. John Perse's "Winds" ("Vents"), a poem about America which suggested the idea of this piece because it was going to be like a constant motion, everything moving all the time and changing. The poem did suggest many aspects of this piece which I vaguely had in mind, and it helped me to work on it—and then I began to find the poem was a little more bombastic than I like. The general plan and the general conception of the poem were a help, but I began to dislike the details and the false primitiveness.

CR

For a number of years your style of writing was associated with something that is called metrical modulation. Would you speak about that particular device and the role it played in your music?

EC

It actually started with the Cello Sonata, and in a sense the opening of the Cello Sonata indicates what this is all about—that is, you hear the cello play as if it were not connected with the piano and as if it had its own pulse and its own kind of motion. Metrical modulation is not very complicated; it is simply an overlapping of one speed with another, and the piece becomes a series of overlappings all the way through. In a work like the Cello Sonata or the First String Quartet you have a sort of basic speed which comes in at the beginning and at the end of the work like a tonic chord—and then the work modulates through many different speeds, all quite smoothly. What I try to do is to give not only the impression of constant motion, but also the sense of the different ways that we experience motion. We always see different kinds of motions going on around us simultaneously—different in character and speed—and I have tried to provide this rather familiar experience in music. In a way, all the composers of the twentieth century, up to the time when I began, had been looking for a way to do this. Stravinsky, by writing music that constantly changed its pattern of rather fast, regular notes with irregular accents achieved a kind of stylized rubato. Schoenberg, on the other hand, wrote music that was like prose—it had no common, basic beat. I was going to write music that combined these two ideas in one, and actually the opening of the Cello Sonata does exactly that.

CR

Previously, the unity of sentiment in music always implied a unity of tempo so that one generally measured out the time in exactly the same units all through the piece; when the tempo changed the emotional complexity or the emotional character changed. In your music, the emotional character comes from the combination of different kinds of tempo, different kinds of time.

EC

Yes, I think it does. I think my music is very much like the kind of thing you see in the moving pictures, in which the camera will show you a big scene, and then focus on one small part of it, and then move over and show you something else. Many of my pieces, like the Concerto for Orchestra, are like this: there is a total world of sound going on, and the form of the piece involves picking out and drawing the attention of the listener to one aspect or another of it, and making the others fade into the background.

This script is based on an interview produced by Misha Donat for the BBC in April 1983.

A Guide to Elliott Carter Research Materials at the Library of Congress Music Division

by Morgan Cundiff

List of Works

1931	Incidental music for Sophocles's *Philoctetes* for baritone, men's chorus, oboe, and percussion
1936	Incidental music for Plautus's *Mostellaria* for baritone, men's chorus, and small orchestra
1936	*Tarantella* (Ovid) (arranged for piano four-hands and men's chorus) from Incidental music for Plautus's *Mostellaria*
1937	*Let's Be Gay* (John Gay), women's voices and piano
1937	*Harvest Home* (Robert Herrick), mixed voices, a cappella
1937	*To Music* (Robert Herrick), mixed voices, a cappella
1938	Prelude, Fanfare and Polka, small orchestra
1938	*Tell Me Where Is Fancy Bred,* Incidental music for *The Merchant of Venice,* guitar and alto voice
1938	*Heart Not So Heavy As Mine* (Emily Dickinson), mixed voices, a cappella
1939	*Pocahontas,* orchestra
1939	Suite from *Pocahontas*
1939	Canoic Suite for Quartet of Alto Saxophones
1940	Pastoral for Viola (or English Horn or Clarinet) and Piano
1941	*The Defense of Corinth* (Rabelais), men's voices, piano four-hands, and speaker
1942	Symphony No. 1
1943	Elegy for Viola (or Cello) and Piano
1943	*Voyage* (Hart Crane), medium voice and piano
1943	*Warble for Lilac Time* (Walt Whitman), soprano or tenor and piano; also arranged for voice and small orchestra
1943	*The Rose Family* (Robert Frost), medium voice and piano
1943	*The Dust of Snow* (Robert Frost), medium voice and piano
1943	*The Line Gang* (Robert Frost), baritone and piano
1944	*The Difference* (Mark van Doren), duet for soprano and barytone
1944	*Holiday* Overture
1944	*The Harmony of Morning* (Mark van Doren), four-part women's voices and chamber orchestra
1945	*Musicians Wrestle Everywhere* (Emily Dickinson), mixed voices, a cappella

1945–46	Piano Sonata (1945-46)
1946	Elegy arranged for string quartet
1947	*The Minotaur*
1947	Suite from *The Minotaur*
1947	*Emblems* (Allen Tate), men's voices and piano
1948	Woodwind Quintet
1948	Sonata for Violoncello and Piano
1949/66	Eight Pieces for Four Timpani (Six written in 1949, revised with two added in 1966)
1949	Eight Etudes and a Fantasy for Woodwind Quartet
1951	String Quartet no. 1
1952	Elegy arranged for string orchestra
1952	Sonata for Flute, Oboe, Cello and Harpsichord
1955	Variations for Orchestra
1956	Canonic Suite for Four Clarinets (arrangement and revision of Canonic Suite for Quartet of Alto Saxophones)
1959	String Quartet no. 2
1959–61	Double Concerto for Harpsichord and Piano with Two Chamber Orchestras
1964–65	Piano Concerto
1969	Concerto for Orchestra
1971	Canon for Three
1971	String Quartet no. 3
1973–74	Duo for Violin and Piano
1974	Brass Quintet
1974	*A Fantasy about Purcell's "Fantasia upon One Note"*
1975	*A Mirror on Which to Dwell* (Elizabeth Bishop), soprano and small chamber orchestra
1976	A Symphony of Three Orchestras
1978	*Syringa* (John Ashbery, Greek texts), mezzo-soprano, baritone, and chamber orchestra
1978	*Birthday Fanfare*
1980	*Night Fantasies*
1980	*Three Poems by Robert Frost (1943)*, arranged for mezzo-soprano and chamber orchestra

1981	*In Sleep, In Thunder* (Robert Lowell), tenor and chamber orchestra
1982	Piano Sonata (1945–46), revised 1982
1982–83	Triple Duo

A Catalog of the Special Collection

All the information within quotation marks appears in the composer's own hand on the manuscripts.

Canon from Easy Piano Pieces "1940?"
  1 p. holograph on transparency
  "unpublished"
  Box 70, Folder 9

Canonic Suite for Four Clarinets
  5 pp. of holograph score on transparencies
  "Revised version of Suite for Four Alto Saxophones
    1945—revised in 1956"
  Box 67, Folder 3

Canonic Suite for Quartet of Alto Saxophones
  printed score, BMI, 1945, 16 pp.
  penciled revisions made in 1954
  Microfilm: MUSIC–1835
  Box 67, Folder 4

Concerto for Orchestra
  photocopy of pp. 1-29 with corrections and revisions
  20 rejected pages
  1 p. diagram "recopied from Dec. 4, 1966—and other
    places—Sept. 1967"
  photocopy of entire score (108 pp.) with revisions
  "Rome—Waccabuc Nov. 25, 1969"
  Box 1

Concerto for Orchestra—Sketches
  216 1.
  contains sketches labeled:
    "chord system pairs"
    "general plan"
    "combinations of each group"
    "coordination of all chords"
  Box 2

Concerto for Orchestra—Sketches
  340 1.
  Box 35

Concerto for Orchestra—Sketches
12 1.
Box 36

Concerto for Orchestra—Sketches
140 1.
Box 37

Concerto for Orchestra—Sketches
280 1.
Box 38

Concerto for Orchestra—Sketches
250 1.
Box 39

Concerto for Orchestra—Sketches
240 1.
Box 40

Concerto for Orchestra—Sketches
183 1.
Box 41

Counterpoint Exercises with Nadia Boulanger, 1933–35
105 1.
Microfilm: MUSIC-1817
Box 65

The Defense of Corinth
holograph score, 49 pp.
"text from Rabelais: Prologue to Book III of Pantagruel,
   translated by Urquhart and Motteux."
For: speaker, 4-part men's chorus, piano 4 hands
"Dedicated to: G. Wallace Woodworth and the Harvard
   Glee Club"
Box 3

The Difference
"Duet for Soprano and Barytone (1944)"
photocopy score, 10 pp. (duration approx. 10 min.)
poem by Mark van Doren, text on p. 10
"Unpublished"
Box 70, Folder 7

Double Concerto for Harpsichord and Piano with Two Chamber
    Orchestras
129 pp.
holograph score on transparencies (in pencil, unbound)
2 pp. of title, instrumentation, stage directions and
    performance instructions
"Commissioned by the Fromm Foundation."
"Duration: about 23 minutes"
"Waccabuc, N.Y. August, 1961"
Box 4

Double Concerto—Sketches
80 pp.
rejected pages, sketches, and 2 rejected staging charts
Microfilm: MUSIC-1813 D
Box 5

Double Concerto—Sketches
205 l.
many diagrams and graphs in different colored pencils
    illustrating rhythmic relationships
Microfilm: MUSIC-1813 D
Box 6

Double Concerto—Sketches
114 l.
various blueprint pages from score with corrections
Microfilm: MUSIC-1813 D
Box 7

Double Concerto—Sketches
photocopy of holograph score pp. 1–37 with pencil
    revisions
Microfilm: MUSIC-1813 D
Box 8

Double Concerto—Sketches
204 l.
Microfilm: MUSIC-1813 B & C
Box 57

Double Concerto—Sketches concerned with piano cadenza
189 l.
Microfilm: MUSIC-1813 B & C
Box 58

Double Concerto—Sketches
   188 l.
   Microfilm: MUSIC-1813 B & C
   Box 59

Double Concerto—Sketches, First version
   184 l.
   Microfilm: MUSIC-1813
   Box 60

Double Concerto—Sketches, First version
   280 l.
   Microfilm: MUSIC-1813
   Box 61

Double Concerto—Sketches
   200 l.
   Microfilm: MUSIC-1813 B & C
   Box 62

Double Concerto—Sketches
   195 l.
   Microfilm: MUSIC-1813 B & C
   Box 63

Double Concerto—Sketches
   140 l.
   Microfilm: MUSIC-1813 B & C
   Box 64

Dust of Snow for voice and piano
   holograph on transparencies, 2 pp.
   poem by Robert Frost
   Box 72, Folder 7

Eight Etudes and a Fantasy for Woodwind Quartet (1950)
   holograph score and parts on transparencies
   score, 28 pp.
   flute part, 11 pp.
   oboe part, 9 pp.
   clarinet part, 11 pp.
   bassoon part, 10 pp.
   "For: Richard Franko Goldman"
   Microfilm: MUSIC-1816
   Box 71, Folder 1

Eight Etudes and a Fantasy
  photocopy of score with pencil and ink revisions
  28 pp.
  Microfilm: MUSIC-1816 C
  Box 71, Folder 3

Eight Etudes and a Fantasy—Sketches
  68 l.
  Microfilm: MUSIC-1816
  Box 71, Folder 2

Eight Pieces for Four Tympani
  "Recitative and Improvisation for Four Kettledrums"
  (from Six Pieces for Kettledrums)
  holograph on transparencies, 5 pp.
  Microfilm: MUSIC-1830
  Box 70, Folder 3

Eight Pieces for Four Tympani
  "Suite for Timpani"
  "Improvisation and Recitative"
  holograph on transparencies, 3 pp.
  "Recitative"
  holograph, 2 pp.
  "Improvisation, March, Recitative"
  photocopy with performer's notes, 5 pp.
  Microfilm: MUSIC-1830
  Box 70, Folder 4

Elegy for Cello and Piano
  "Adagio for Cello and Piano"
  holograph score on transparencies
  3 pp. score, 1 p. cello part
  "arranged from Adagio for Viola and Piano"
  Microfilm: MUSIC-1814 C
  Box 69, Folder 10

Elegy for String Quartet
  "for the Lanier String Quartet"
  pencil holograph score, 2 pp.
  ink holograph score on transparencies, 4 pp.
  holograph parts on transparencies, 1 p. each
  Microfilm: MUSIC-1814 C
  Box 69, Folder 8

Elegy for String Quartet
   to the Lanier Quartet, 2 pp. photostat
   "transcription of original cello piece"
   Adagio for Cello and Piano (1944)
   holograph score, 3 pp.
   "Original piece—later transcribed for:
      a) viola and piano
      b) string quartet
      c) string orchestra
      d) rewritten for viola (1961?) E.C."
   Adagio for Viola and Piano
   photocopy score
   "From 'cello and piano original, E.C.
      old version of viola transcription rewritten in
      (1965?) and published by PEER INT."
   Microfilm: MUSIC-1814 C
   Box 69, Folder 11

Elegy for String Quartet—Sketches
   2 pp.
   "Sept. 1961 revision of Elegy"
   Microfilm: MUSIC-1814
   Box 69, Folder 12

Elegy for Viola and Piano
   "Adagio for Viola and Piano (1944)"
   holograph on transparencies
   score 3 pp., viola part 1 p.
   "original version"
   also photocopy of score with pencil revisions, 3 pp.
   "revision 1961"
   Microfilm: MUSIC-1814 A
   Box 69, Folder 7

Elegy for Viola and Piano
   1943 revised 1961
   holograph score on transparencies, 3 pp.
   also contains 3 pp. of sketches of same piece
   Microfilm: MUSIC-1814 B
   Box 69, Folder 9

Emblems
   holograph score, 35 pp. unbound
   for 4-part men's chorus (TTBB) and piano solo
   Poems by Allen Tate
   "To: G. Wallace Woodworth and Harvard Glee Club"

"Dorset, Vt. Sept., 1947"
Microfilm: MUSIC-1815 B
Box 9

Emblems
99 l.
Microfilm: MUSIC-1815 A
Box 73, Folder 1

Exercises and Studies
54 pp., unbound
harmony, counterpoint, melody, and stylistic exercises for students
Box 67, Folder 7

Folk Dance no. 2—Sketch
1 p.
Box 71, Folder 5

Harvest Home
holograph score on transparencies, 14 pp.
for chorus a cappella (SSATB)
poem by Robert Herrick
"1937-8(?) same time as *To Music*"
Box 70, Folder 1

Holiday Overture
holograph score, 69 pp., unbound
For orchestra: duration 9½ minutes
"This work is the winning composition in a competition
    sponsored by Independent Music Publishers, New York City, in
    1945"
"Saltaire, L.I. August, 1944"
Microfilm: MUSIC-1818 B
Box 10

Holiday Overture
1 p. holograph transparency, meas. 31-38
"revision of these measures (from 1944 score)"
"unpublished"
Box 70, Folder 8

Holiday Overture—Sketches
22 l.
Microfilm: MUSIC-1818A
Box 11

Invention: See Sketchbook

Labyrinth: See Sketchbook

Let's Be Gay
  holograph score on transparencies, 9 pp.
  for SSA and 2 pianos
  Words by John Gay
  "unpublished—1938–39"
  Box 67, Folder 6

Let's Be Gay
  holograph choral score on transparencies, 4 pp.
  Box 67, Folder 5

The Minotaur Ballet in One Act
  holograph on transparencies of "Orchestra score of Complete Version," 194 pp., unbound
  "to Lincoln Kirstein"
  "NYC March 13, 1947"
  Box 71, Folder 4

The Minotaur—Sketches
  50 l.
  Microfilm: MUSIC-1819
  Box 12

Minotaur: See also Sketchbook

"Mostellaria music (1936?)"—Sketches
  12 l., bound in exercise book
  Box 68, Folder 5

Music for Sophocles's Philoctetes
  mimeographed chorus part, 17 pp.
  for men's chorus accompanied by oboe and percussion
  text in Greek
  "given by Harvard Classical Club 1934 or 5?"
  Box 72, Folder 5

Musicians Wrestle Everywhere
  photocopy of score with corrections, 17 pp.
  Madrigal for 5-part chorus (SSATB)
  with string orchestra accompaniment
  poem by Emily Dickinson
  Microfilm: MUSIC-1820

Pastoral for English Horn and Piano or Viola and Piano (1940)
　holograph score on transparencies, 12 pp.
　Microfilm: MUSIC-1822 B
　Box 72, Folder 1

Pastoral for English Horn and Piano
　2 photocopies of score, 12 pp. each
　Microfilm: MUSIC-1822 A
　Box 72, Folder 4

Pastoral for Piano and Viola (English Horn or Clarinet)
　corrected proofs
　piano part, 15 pp.
　viola, English horn, and clarinet parts, 4 pp. each
　Microfilm: MUSIC-1822 B
　Box 72, Folder 2

Pastoral for Piano and Viola
　photocopy of English horn version with attached transpositions for
　　viola, 12 pp.
　also contains English horn part and viola part, 5 pp. each
　Microfilm: MUSIC-1822 A
　Box 72, Folder 3

Piano Concerto
　holograph score on transparencies, 118 pp., unbound
　For piano and orchestra
　"Dedicated to Igor Stravinsky on his 85th birthday with
　　great admiration and friendship."
　"Commissioned by Jacob Lateiner through the Ford Foundation."
　Contains instrumentation page with stage directions.
　"Berlin, Waccabuc September, 1965"
　Box 13

Piano Concerto
　holograph on transparency of p. 54 of score
　Box 86

Piano Concerto—Sketches
　233 l.
　Microfilm: MUSIC-1836
　Box 42

Piano Concerto—Sketches
　172 l.
　Microfilm: MUSIC-1836
　Box 43

Piano Concerto—Sketches
173 l.
Microfilm: MUSIC-1836
Box 44

Piano Concerto—Sketches
199 l.
Microfilm: MUSIC-1836
Box 45

Piano Concerto—Sketches
280 l.
Microfilm: MUSIC-1836
Box 46

Piano Concerto—Sketches
370 l.
Microfilm: MUSIC-1836
Box 47

Piano Concerto—Sketches
412 l.
Microfilm: MUSIC-1836
Box 48

Piano Concerto—Sketches
415 l.
Microfilm: MUSIC-1836
Box 49

Piano Concerto—Sketches
223 l.
Microfilm: MUSIC-1836
Box 50

Piano Concerto—Sketches
299 l.
Microfilm: MUSIC-1836
Box 51

Piano Concerto—Sketches
241 l.
Microfilm: MUSIC-1836
Box 52

Piano Concerto—Sketches
   236 l.
   Microfilm: MUSIC-1836
   Box 53

Piano Concerto—Sketches
   213 l.
   Microfilm: MUSIC-1836
   Box 54

Piano Concerto—Sketches
   217 l.
   Microfilm: MUSIC-1836
   Box 55

Piano Concerto—Sketches
   76 l.
   Microfilm: MUSIC-1836
   Box 56

Piano Concerto—Sketches
   2 pp.
   Microfilm: MUSIC-1836
   Box 67, Folder 8

Piano Sonata 1945–46
   holograph score on transparencies, 34 pp., unbound
   Microfilm: MUSIC-1828 B
   Box 14

Piano Sonata
   photocopy score, 34 pp. spiral notebook, pencil
   "Early copy with corrections in pencil and red ink"
   "Truro, New York   Jan. 1946"
   Microfilm: MUSIC-1828 C
   Box 15

Piano Sonata (1945-46)
   photocopy of holograph score with manuscript
   also contains publisher's second proof of leaves 24-44
   Microfilm: MUSIC-1828
   Box 69, Folder 1

Piano Sonata—Sketches
115 1.
Microfilm: MUSIC-1828 A
Box 16

Piano Trio (uncompleted)—Sketches
38 1.
Box 67, Folder 10

Pocahontas
incomplete score for 2 pianos
23 1., pencil
Box 17

Pocahontas—"1st version incomplete"
holograph, 14 1.
for keyboard
Microfilm: MUSIC-1821
Box 69, Folder 4

Pocahontas
holograph orchestral score
29 1., incomplete
Microfilm: MUSIC-1821
Box 69, Folder 5

Pocahontas—Sketches
9 1.
Microfilm: MUSIC-1821
Box 69, Folder 3

Prelude, Fanfare and Polka
for flute, oboe, bass clarinet, alto saxophone, tenor
saxophone, strings
photocopy, 29 pp., bound
"Composer's facsimile edition copyright 1952"
"Unpublished"
Box 70, Folder 6

The Rose Family for voice and piano
holograph on transparencies, 2 pp.
poem by Robert Frost
Box 72, Folder 6

Sketchbook
    bound, no date
    contains *Labyrinth* for 4 muted trumpets or 4 horns, 3 pp.
    "4 part canon at unison written in Paris"
    Invention—theme by Prout, 3 parts, 2 pp.
    Box 68, Folder 1

Sketchbook, date uncertain
    easy pieces, counterpoint exercises
    Minotaur sketches, rounds
    Box 68, Folder 2

Sketchbook
    Two Fanfares for Brass Ensemble and Percussion
        (4 horns, 3 trumpets, 3 trombones, tuba, timpani)
    also contains "counterpoint—Paris" exercises
    short sketch for piece for chorus with percussion
    "chorus? (text by Auden? Dog beneath the skin?)"
        "Fanfares—date—later in 40's?"
    Box 68, Folder 3

Sonata for Flute, Oboe, Cello and Harpsichord—Sketches
    28 l.
    Microfilm: MUSIC-1827
    Box 73, Folder 2

Sonata for Violoncello and Piano
    holograph on transparencies
    cello part, 14 pp.
    "To Bernard Greenhouse"
    "Dec. 11, 1948 Dorset, Vt.—N.Y."
    Microfilm: MUSIC-1829 B
    Box 18

Sonata for Violoncello and Piano—Sketches
    41 pp., photocopy, spiral bound
    "First copy with pencil corrections"
    "Dec. 11, 1948 Dorset, Vt.—N.Y."
    Microfilm: MUSIC-1829 C
    Box 19

Sonata for Violoncello and Piano—Sketches
    170 l.
    Microfilm: MUSIC-1829 A
    Box 20

String Quartet no. 1
   holograph score on transparencies, 101 pp.
   +1 p. "notes on notation" unbound
   "Tucson—Dorset Sept. 1951"
   Microfilm: MUSIC-1824 B
   Box 24

String Quartet no. 1
   3 copies of Composer's Facsimile Edition with pencil
     corrections
   "To: The Walden Quartet"
   Microfilm: MUSIC-1824 B
   Box 25

String Quartet no. 2
   holograph score on transparencies with pencil corrections,
     59 pp. +1 p. Prefatory Note
   "To the Stanley Quartet"
   Duration: "about 20 minutes"
   "Waccabuc June 3, 1959"
   Microfilm: MUSIC-1825 B
   Box 26

String Quartet no. 3—Sketches
   210 l.
   Box 30

String Quartet no. 3—Sketches
   311 l.
   Box 31

String Quartet no. 3—Sketches
   285 l.
   Box 32

String Quartet no. 3—Sketches
   221 l.
   Box 33

String Quartet no. 3—Sketches
   181 l.
   Box 34

String Quartet no. 1—Sketches
259 1.
Microfilm: MUSIC-1824 A
Box 66

String Quartet no. 1—Sketches
16 pp., pencil
"A few sketches made before hitting on Quartet 1950-51"
Box 70, Folder 5

Symphony No. 1
holograph score on transparencies, 139 pp., unbound
"slightly revised 1954"
"Santa Fe, N.M. Dec. 19, 1942"
Microfilm: MUSIC-1831 B
Box 21

Symphony No. 1
photocopy of score with corrections
"To My Wife"
Microfilm: MUSIC-1831 C
Box 22

Symphony No. 1—Sketches
90 1.
Microfilm: MUSIC-1831 A
Box 23

Symphony No. 1—Sketchbook
17 1., 3 x 5 in.
Box 67, Folder 9

Tarantella from Ovid's *Fasti*
holograph score, 38 pp., very poor condition
"Ovid's Festivalls (or Romane Calendar)
Translated by John Gower, London 1640"
"For 4-part men's chorus and orchestra (1936) from
Incidental Music to Pautus' *Mostellaria* (arranged for
chamber orchestra)"
Box 27, Folder 1

Tarantella from Ovid's *Fasti*
2 versions
holograph, bound score, 23 l.
for flute, clarinet, trumpet, 2 pianos, chorus TTBB, strings
holograph score, unbound, 25 pp.
2 pianos, chorus TTBB
Box 68, Folder 4

Tarantella—Sketch for orchestration—1937
holograph, 38 pp.
Box 27, Folder 2

Tell Me Where Is Fancy Bred 1936 (Shakespeare) for Voice
Guitar and Piano
photocopy of score, 5 pp.
Microfilm: MUSIC-1832
Box 69, Folder 2

To Music
holograph score on transparencies, 12 pp., unbound
words by Robert Herrick
Box 67, Folder 2

To Music—chorus parts
holographs on transparencies
soprano part, 3 pp.
alto part, 3 pp.
tenor part, 3 pp.
bass part, 2 pp.
Box 67, Folder 1

Two Fanfares: See Sketchbook

Variations for Orchestra
holograph score on transparencies, 119 pp., unbound
"Rome—Dorset—N.Y. Finished Nov. 14, 1955"
Microfilm: MUSIC-1833 B
Box 28

Variations for Orchestra—Sketches
780 l.
Microfilm: MUSIC-1833 A
Box 29

Voyage for voice and piano
   holograph on transparencies, 7 pp.
   poem by Hart Crane
   Box 72, Folder 8

Warble for Lilac Time for voice and piano
   holograph on transparencies, 12 pp.
   poem by Walt Whitman from *Autumn Rivulets*
   "copy 1 1st version, 2nd version published"
   Microfilm: MUSIC-1834
   Box 72, Folder 9

Warble for Lilac Time
   holograph on transparencies, 12 pp.
   "copy 2 1st version, 2nd version published"
   "1942 version—revised for publication in 1955"
   Microfilm: MUSIC-1834
   Box 72, Folder 10

Warble for Lilac Time
   photocopy with pencil revisions and paste-over revisions
   12 pp.
   Microfilm: MUSIC-1834
   Box 72, Folder 11

Woodwind Quintet
   holograph score on transparencies, 14 pp.
   "To Mademoiselle Nadia Boulanger"
   Box 73, Folder 6

Woodwind Quintet—parts
   flute part, 3 pp.
   oboe part, 3 pp.
   clarinet part, 3 pp.
   bassoon part, 3 pp.
   horn part, 2 pp.
      (all parts holograph transparencies)
   also contains 2 pp. of holograph score on transparencies
      (from second movement with corrections)
   Microfilm: MUSIC-1826
   Box 73, Folder 3

Woodwind Quintet—Sketches
   56 l.
   Microfilm: MUSIC-1826
   Box 73, Folder 4

Woodwind Quintet—Sketches
14 l.
Microfilm: MUSIC-1826
Box 73, Folder 5

Library of Congress Performances

The following is an alphabetical list of performances of Elliott Carter's music which have taken place in the Coolidge Auditorium of the Library of Congress. The last name in the entry indicates the donor under whose auspices the concert was funded.

All of the concerts were recorded and can be heard in the Library's Performing Arts Reading Room. The Recording Laboratory will provide copies of the tapes for a nominal fee, provided that the order is accompanied by written permission from the composer or copyright holder and the performers. Inquires about availability and cost should be addressed to Recording Laboratory, Library of Congress, Washington, D.C. 20540.

The Defense of Corinth, for men's chorus, narrator, and two pianos (1941)
    The Hofstader Singers
    Robert Hofstader, conductor
    Salvador Thomas, narrator
    Jean Wentworth, piano
    Kenneth Wentworth, piano
November 28, 1952   Coolidge

Double Concerto for Harpsichord and Piano with Two Chamber Orchestras (1959-61)
    The Contemporary Chamber Ensemble
    Arthur Weisberg, conductor
    Paul Jacobs, harpsichord
    Gilbert Kalish, piano
February 8, 1974   Whittall

Duo for Violin and Piano (1973–74)
    Paul Zukofsky, violin
    Ursula Oppens, piano
September 29, 1977   Koussevitzky and McKim

Duo for Violin and Piano (1973–74)
    Paul Zukofsky, violin
    Gilbert Kalish, piano
February 27, 1976
October 7, 1978   McKim

Eight Etudes and a Fantasy for Woodwind Quartet (1949)
    New York Woodwind Quintet
    Samuel Baron, flute

Jerome Roth, oboe
David Glazer, clarinet
Arthur Weisberg, bassoon
January 27, 1961   Whittall

Elegy for Viola and Piano (1943)
Samuel Rhodes, viola
Gilbert Kalish, piano
October 7, 1978   Elson and McKim

Etudes and a Fantasy from Eight Etudes and a Fantasy for Woodwind
Quartets (1949)
Nos. 1, 4, 5, 6, 8, and Fantasy only.
Mozarteum Woodwind Quintet of Argentina
Alfreddo Ianelli, flute
Mariano Frogioni, clarinet
Pedro Pablo Cocchiararo, oboe
Pedro J. Chiambaretta, bassoon
February 6, 1970   Coolidge

A Mirror on Which to Dwell for soprano and small chamber orchestra
(1975)
The Contemporary Chamber Ensemble
Arthur Weisberg, musical director
Susan Belling, soprano
March 9, 1979   Coolidge

Pastoral for Viola and Piano (1940)
Samuel Rhodes, viola
Gilbert Kalish, piano
October 7, 1978   Elson and McKim

Piano Sonata (1945-46)
Charles Rosen, piano and lecturer
October 7, 1978   Elson and McKim

Sonata for Flute, Oboe, Cello, and Harpsichord (1952)
New York Chamber Soloists
Samuel Baron, flute
Melvin Kaplan, oboe
Alexander Kouguell, cello
Harriet Wingreen, harpsichord
January 31, 1964   Whittall

Sonata for Violoncello and Piano (1948)
   Michael Rudiakov, cello
   Richard Goode, piano
March 4, 1977   McKim
   Joel Krosnick, cello
   Gilbert Kalish, piano
October 7, 1978   Elson and McKim
   Bernard Greenhouse, cello
   Manahem Pressler, piano
January 4, 1974   Whittall

String Quartet no. 1 (1951)
   The Walden String Quartet
   Homer Schmitt, Bernard Goodman, violins
   John Garvey, viola
   Robert Swenson, cello
January 28, 1955   Coolidge

String Quartet no. 2 (1959)
   The Juilliard Quartet
   Robert Mann, Isidore Cohen, violins
   Raphael Hillyer, viola
   Claus Adam, cello
October 30, 1960   Coolidge

String Quartet no. 2 (1959)
   The Juilliard Quartet
   Robert Mann, Isidore Cohen, violins
   Raphael Hillyer, viola
   Claus Adam, cello
October 10 and 11, 1962
April 18 and 19, 1968   Whittall
   The Juilliard Quartet
   Robert Mann, Earl Carlyss, violins
   Samuel Rhodes, viola
   Joel Krosnick, cello
April 27 and 28, 1978   Whittall

String Quartet No. 2 (1959)
   The Juilliard Quartet
   Robert Mann, Earl Carlyss, violins
   Samuel Rhodes, viola
   Joel Krosnick, cello
April 27 and 28, 1978   Whittall

String Quartet no. 2 (1959)
  The Juilliard Quartet
  Robert Mann, Earl Carlyss, violins
  Samuel Rhodes, viola
  Joel Krosnick, cello
October 7, 1978   Elson and McKim

String Quartet no. 3 (1971)
  The Juilliard Quartet
  Robert Mann, Earl Carlyss, violins
  Samuel Rhodes, viola
  Claus Adam, cello
April 26 and 27, 1973   Whittall
  The Juilliard Quartet
  Robert Mann, Earl Carlyss, violins
  Samuel Rhodes, viola
  Joel Krosnick, cello
November 6 and 7, 1975   Whittall

Woodwind Quintet (1948)
  New York Woodwind Quintet
  Samuel Baron, flute
  Ronald Roseman, oboe
  David Glazer, clarinet
  Arthur Weisberg, bassoon
  Ralph Froelich, French horn
March 3, 1967   Whittall

Woodwind Quintet (1948)
  Dorian Quintet
  Karl Kraber, flute
  Charles Kuskin, oboe
  William Lewis, clarinet
  Jane Taylor, bassoon
  Barry Benjamin, French horn
December 5, 1969   Coolidge

Woodwind Quintet (1948)
  The Festival Winds
  John Solum, flute
  Melvin Kaplan, oboe
  Charles Russo, clarinet
  Arthur Weisberg, bassoon
  Ralph Froelich, French horn
January 29, 1971   Whittall

Bibliography

Writings by Elliott Carter

Flawed Words and Stubborn Sounds: A Conversation with Elliott Carter by Allen Edwards (New York: W. W. Norton, 1971).

"In Memory of Richard Franko Goldman," *American Music Center Newsletter* 22, no. 4 (Fall 1980): 13.

Liner notes for recording of *Night Fantasies* and Piano Sonata performed by Paul Jacobs. Nonesuch 79047.

"On Edgard Varèse," *The New Worlds of Edgard Varèse,* ed. Sherman Van Solkema (New York: Institute for Studies in American Music, 1979), pp. 1-8.

"Un Paso Adelante," *Buenos Aires Musical* (December 1959): 63-67.

"Was ist amerikanische Musik?" *Oesterreichische Musik Zeitschrift* 138 (June–August 1978): 61.

The Writings of Elliott Carter, compiled and annotated by Else and Kurt Stone (Bloomington: Indian University Press, 1977). See "articles not included in this edition," pp. 369-70.

Writings About Elliott Carter

Martin Boykan, "Elliott Carter and Postwar Composers," *Perspectives of New Music* 2, no. 2 (Spring–Summer 1964): 125-28.

W. E. Brandt, "The Music of Elliott Carter: Simultaneity and Complexity," *Music Educators Journal* 60 (May 1974): 24-32.

"Carter's 'Musical Problems'," *Broadcast Music Inc.* (May 1971): 23.

Andrew Clements, "Elliott Carter Views American Music," *Music and Musicians* 26, no. 7 (March 1978): 32-34.

Arthur Cohn, "His Own Man — the Music of Elliott Carter," *American Record Guide* 37, no. 11 (July 1971): 756-59.

"Composer Elliott Carter Interviewed," *Chicago Tribune,* Section 6 (April 8, 1979): 9.

Aaron Copland, "Presentation to Elliott C. Carter of the Gold Medal for Music," *Proceedings of the American Academy of Arts and Letters and the National Institute of Arts and Letters,* 2nd series, no. 22 (1972), pp. 32–33.

Andrew DeRhen, "League-ISCM: Carter Works," *High Fidelity–Musical America* 29 (February 1979): MA 22–24.

"Elite Composer," *Time* 67, no. 22 (May 28, 1956): 48.

"Elliott Carter," *Composers of the Americas* 5 (1959): 29–35.

"Elliott Carter" *in* "Contributors to This Issue," *Score* 12 (June 1955): 94.

Elliott Carter: A 70th Birthday Tribute (London: G. Schirmer, 1978).

Ray E. Ellsworth, "Classic Modern," *Down Beat* 24, no. 19 (September 19, 1957): 36.

Raymond Ericson, "Carter on the Record," *New York Times* (February 1, 1970).

David Ewen, *Composers Since 1900: A Biographical and Critical Guide* (New York: H. W. Wilson, 1969), pp. 116–19.

William Flanagan, "Elliott Carter, " *The International Cyclopedia of Music and Musicians,* ed. in chief Oscar Thompson, ed. ninth edition, Robert Sabin (New York: Dodd, Mead, 1964) pp. 345–46.

Shirley Fleming, "The Composer's String Quartet Conducts a Competition," *High Fidelity–Musical America* 24 (August 1974): MA 19.

Cole Gagne and Tracy Caras, *Soundpieces: Interviews with American Composers* (Metuchen: Scarecrow, 1982).

Peggy Granville-Hicks, "Elliott Carter," *Grove's Dictionary of Music and Musicians,* fifth edition, ed. Eric Blom (New York: St. Martin's, 1955) pp. 97–98.

_____ *Grove's* . . . Supplement (New York: St. Martin's, 1961) pp. 63–64.

Richard Franko Goldman, "Current Chronicle," *Musical Quarterly* 37, no. 1 (January 1951): 83–89.

_____ "The Music of Elliott Carter," *Musical Quarterly* 43, no. 2 (April 1957): 151–70.

P. Griffiths, "Twentieth Century," *Musical Times* 115 (February 1974): 153–55.

David Hamilton, "American Pioneers of the New Music," *High Fidelity–Musical America* 18 (September 1968): 47.

_____ *The Nation* 222 (March 1976): 382.

Charles Hamm, *Music in the New World* (New York: Norton, 1983), pp. 567–71.

Robert Hurwitz, "Elliott Carter: The Communication of Time," *Changes in the Arts* 78 (November 1972): 10–11.

Adrian Jack, "Modern," *Music and Musicians* 22 (February 24, 1974): 44–47.

Richard Jackson, ed., *Elliott Carter: Sketches and Scores in Manuscript* (New York: New York Public Library, 1973).

Elod Juhasz, "Husz nap Salzburgban," *Muszika* 19, no. 7 (July 1976): 11-13.

Sheila Keats, "Reference Articles on American Composers: An Index," *Juilliard Review* 1, no. 3 (Fall 1954): 24.

Leighton Kerner, "Creators on Creating: Elliott Carter," *Saturday Review* 7 (December 1980): 38–42.

_____ "Elliott Carter Wrestles at 70," *Village Voice* (December 25, 1978): 87–88.

_____ "The Eloquence of Elliott Carter," *Village Voice* (November 11, 1974).

Horst Koegler, "Blick in die Welt," *Musica* 12, no. 6 (June 1958): 363.

_____ "Europäer hören amerikanische Musik," *Der Monat* 10, no. 117 (June 1958): 68–73.

_____ "Begegungen mit Elliott Carter," *Melos* 26 (1959): 256–58.

Irving Kolodin, "Evenings with Carter, Rubinstein, and Barber," *Saturday Review* 2 (March 22, 1975): 33.

Richard Kostelanetz, "The Astounding Success of Elliott Carter," *High Fidelity* 18, no. 5 (May 1968): 41–45.

_____ *Master Minds: Portraits of Contemporary American Artists and Intellectuals* (New York: Macmillan, 1969), pp. 289–303.

A. Kozinn, *Fugue* 3 (April 1979): 32–36.

Joseph Machlis, *Introduction to Contemporary Music* (New York: W. W. Norton, 1961), pp. 588–96.

Wilfred Mellers, *Music in a New Found Land* (New York: Alfred A. Knopf, 1965), pp. 102–21.

Orin Moe, "The Music of Elliott Carter," *College Music Symposium* 22, no. 1 (Spring 1982): 7–31.

Robert P. Morgan, "The Musician's Dialogue," *The Nation* (December 10, 1977): 630.

Bayan Northcott, "Carter in Perspective," *Musical Times* 119 (December 1978): 1039–41.

_____ "Elliott Carter—Continuity and Coherence," *Music and Musicians* 20, no. 12 (August 1972): 28–39.

G. Potvin, "Seven Leading Composers Look at Music of Today and Its Public," *Music Scene* 37, no. 2 (September–October 1967): 5.

"A Prestigious German Award for Elliott Carter (Ernst von Siemens Music Prize)," *Symphony Magazine* 32 (1981): 113–14.

Ned Rorem, "Elliott Carter," *New Republic* 166 (February 25, 1972): 22. Reprinted in *Pure Contraption* (New York: Holt, Rinehart, and Winston, 1974), pp. 23–26.

_____ "Messiaen and Carter on Their Birthdays," *Tempo*, no. 127 (December 1978): 22–24.

Charles Rosen, "Elliott Carter," *Dictionary of Contemporary Music,* ed. John Vinton (New York: Dutton, 1974), pp. 127–29.

Paul Rosenfeld, "The Newest American Composers," *Modern Music* 15, no. 3 (March–April 1938): 157–58.

Eric Salzman, *Twentieth-Century Music: An Introduction* (Englewood Cliffs, N.J.: Prentice-Hall, 1967), pp. 172–73.

_____ "Unity in Variety," *New York Times* 109 (March 20, 1960): 9.

Lazare Saminsky, *Living Music of the Americas* (New York: Howell, Soskin and Crown, 1949), pp. 92–94.

Valerie Scher, "Composers Quartet and the Complex Music of Elliott Carter," *Chicago Sun-Times* (April 12, 1979).

David Schiff, "Carter in the Seventies," *Tempo* 130 (September 1979): 2–10.

_____ *The Music of Elliott Carter* (London: Eulenburg, 1983).

Lloyd Schwartz, "Elliott Carter Hears the Music in Words," *Boston After Dark* (December 6, 1977).

Abraham Skulsky, "Elliott Carter," *Bulletin of American Composers Alliance* 3, no. 2 (Summer 1953): 2–16.

_____ "The High Cost of Creativity," *Hi-Fi Review* 2, no. 5 (May 1959): 31–36.

Patrick J. Smith, "Elliott Carter, Musician of the Month," *High Fidelity-Musical America* 23, no. 8 (August 1973): MA4–MA5.

Michael Steinberg, "Elliott Carter: An American Original at 70," *Keynote* 2, no. 10 (December 1978): 8–14.

Kurt Stone, "Problems and Methods of Notation," *Perspectives of New Music* 1, no. 2 (Spring 1963): 9–26.

_____ "Current Chronicle: New York," *Musical Quarterly* 55, no. 4 (October 1969): 559–72.

L. Trimble, "Elliott Carter," *Stereo Review* 29 (December 1972): 64–72.

Roman Vlad, "Elliott sic Carter," *La Rassegna musicale* 24, no. 4 (October–December 1954): 369–71.

Jerome F. Weber, *Carter and Schuman* (Utica, N.Y.: J. F. Weber, 1978).

Harold Whipple, "An Elliott Carter Discography," *Perspectives of New Music* (Fall–Winter 1981, Spring–Summer 1982): 169–81.

Arnold Whitthall, "Elliott Carter," *First American Music Conference, Keele University, England, April 18–21, 1975* (Keele: University of Keele, 1977).
_____ *Tempo,* no. 124 (March 1978): 40–43.

Writings About Individual Works

Brass Quintet

P. Griffiths, *Musical Times* 115 (December 1974): 1069.

David Hamilton, *The Nation* (January 11, 1975).

Leighton Kerner, "Solid Gold Chamber Music," *Village Voice* (January 13, 1975).

Bruce Saylor, "American Brass Quintet: Carter," *High Fidelity-Musical America* 24 (August 1974): MA 19.

Canon for 3

Thomas DeLio, "Spatial Design in Elliott Carter's 'Canon for 3'," *Indiana Theory Review* 4, no. 1 (1980): 1-12.

"In Memoriam Igor Stravinsky," *Tempo,* no. 98 (1972): 22-23.

Concerto for Orchestra

Cleveland Orchestra, 486 (January 21, 1971): 93.

Jon Cott, *Rolling Stone* (April 15, 1971).

P. Griffiths, *Musical Times* 116 (October 1975): 894–95.

David Hamilton, *The Nation* 210 (March 2, 1970): 253–54.

_____ *High Fidelity* 20, no. 5 (May 1970): 22.

_____ "Carter's Concerto for Orchestra, a Gripping Musical Experience," *High Fidelity* 21, no. 3 (March 1971): 82.

Robert Jacobson, *Saturday Review* 53 (February 21, 1970): 50.

M. Kastendieck, *American Musical Digest* 1, no. 5 (1970): 23.

Nicholas Kenyon, *Music and Musicians* 24 (October 1975): 50.

Stanley Sadie, *The Times* (London) (August 11, 1972).

Harold Schonberg, *New York Times* (February 6, 1970).

Desmond Shawe-Taylor, "Flux and Turmoil," *New Yorker* 49, no. 52 (February 18, 1974): 104–6.

Patrick J. Smith, *High Fidelity–Musical America* 20, no. 5 (May 1970): 21, 24 (section 2).

Michael Steinberg, *Boston Globe* (February 15, 1970).

The Defense of Corinth

Jacob Avshalomoff, *Notes* 7, no. 3 (June 1950): 442–43.

Arthur Berger, *New York Herald Tribune* (December 19, 1951).

Francis D. Perkins, *New York Herald Tribune* (April 6, 1942).

Cecil Smith, *Musical America* 70 (August 1950): 29.

Alexander Williams, *Boston Herald* (March 13, 1942).

Double Concerto for Harpsichord and Piano with Two Chamber Orchestras

"American Concerto Given First U.K. Performance," *The Times* (London) (April 27, 1962).

Bruce Archibald, "Reviews of Records," *Musical Quarterly* 63, no. 2 (April 1977): 287–89.

Ronald Eyer, *New York Herald Tribune* (September 7, 1961).

A. Frankenstein, *High Fidelity-Musical America* 19 (August 1969): MA 12.

David Fuller, *Notes* 22, no. 1 (Fall 1965): 819–20.

Peter Gorner, *Chicago Tribune* (November 17, 1968).

D. Hamilton, *High Fidelity-Musical America* 17 (February 1967): 85.

David Hamilton, *The Nation* 218, no. 3 (January 19, 1974): 93–94.

Max Harrison, *The Times* (London) (July 31, 1970).

Donal Henahan, *New York Times* (January 24, 1972).

R. Henderson, *Music and Musicians* 14 (January 1966): 20–23.

Alan Rich, *New York Times* (July 22, 1962).

Charles Rosen, *New York Review of Books* 20, no. 2 (February 22, 1973): 25–29.

Eric Salzman, *New York Times* (September 7, 1961).

Arnold Whittall, *Royal Music Association* 94 (1967–68): 12–16.

Carolyn Wilson, *Records and Recording* 11, no. 5 (February 1968): 21–23.

Duo for Violin and Piano

Richard Derby, "Carter's 'Duo for Violin and Piano'," *Perspectives of New Music* (Fall–Winter 1981, Spring–Summer 1982): 149–68.

Music Journal 33 (April 1975): 34.

Andrew Porter, *New Yorker* 51 (April 7, 1975): 129–30.

Eight Etudes and a Fantasy for Woodwind Quartet

Robert Cogan, "Carter's Pair o' Diamonds" Paper for the National Conference on Music Theory, Boston (March 1976).

Ronald Eyer, *Musical America* 72, no. 14 (November 15, 1952): 8.

Alfred Frankenstein, *High Fidelity* 8, no. 5 (May 1958): 54.

Jay S. Harrison, *New York Herald Tribune* (October 29, 1952).

Eight Pieces for Four Timpani

Geary H. Larrick, *Percussionist* 12, no. 1 (Fall 1974).

Robert P. McCormick, *Percussionist* 12, no. 1 (Fall 1974).

"Percussion Volume 2," *Harmonie*, no. 138 (June–August 1978): 61.

The Harmony of Morning
Ruth Douglass, *Notes* 12, no. 3 (June 1955).
Robert Sabin, *Musical America* 75 (June 1955):28.
Virgil Thomas, *New York Herald Tribune* (February 27, 1945).

Holiday Overture
Louis Biancolli, *New York World-Telegram* (April 19, 1960).
Richard Franko Goldman, "Current Chronicle: New York," *Musical Quarterly* 36, no. 4 (July 1950):446-47.
Karl Kroeger, *Notes* 20, no. 3 (Summer 1963):407.
Paul Henry Lang, *New York Herald Tribune* (April 26, 1957).
A. Orga, *Music and Musicians* 16 (December 1967):46.
Peter Stadlen, *London Daily Telegraph* (September 30, 1967).

In Sleep, In Thunder
Roger Heaton, *Tempo*, no. 144 (March 1983):28-29.
David Schiff, " 'In Sleep, In Thunder': Elliott Carter's Portrait of Robert Lowell," *Tempo*, no. 142 (September 1982):2-9.

The Minotaur
Arthur Berger, *New York Herald Tribune* (March 28, 1947).
_____ *New York Herald Tribune* (May 19, 1947).
David Burrows, *The New Haven Symphony Orchestra* (March 6, 1962):8-16.
Cecil Smith, "Sights and Sounds of Spring," *Theatre Arts* 31, no. 6 (June 1947):34.
Walter Terry, *New York Herald* (April 6, 1947).
Douglas Watt, *New Yorker* 32 (May 26, 1956):120-21.

A Mirror on Which to Dwell
Andrew Clements, "UK Premiere for Carter," *Music and Musicians* 24 (December 1976):4.
Andrew DeRhen, "Speculum Musicae: Carter Premiere," *High Fidelity-Musical America* 26 (June 1976):MA 27.
David Hamilton, "Elliott Carter's Contributions to the American Bicentennial" *High Fidelity-Musical America* 31 (August 1981):52.
Leighton Kerner, "Carter Reclaims the Voice for the Mind," *Village Voice* (March 8, 1976):76.
Andrew Porter, "Reflections," *New Yorker* 52 (March 8, 1976):122.

_____ *New Yorker* 53 (March 7, 1977):101-4.

David Schiff, "Elliott Carter: 'A Mirror on Which to Dwell'," *New York Arts Journal* (Spring 1977).

Brigette Schiffer, *Schweizerische Musik Zeitung* 117 (January–February 1977):36.

Musicians Wrestle Everywhere

Virgil Thomson, *New York Herald Tribune* (January 16, 1951).

Night Fantasies

Paul Jacobs, Liner notes for recording of "Night Fantasies" and "Piano Sonata" performed by Paul Jacobs. Nonesuch 79047.

Leighton Kerner, "Music: Carter's Dream-Road," *Village Voice* 26 (November 25, 1981):80.

J. McInerney, "Paul Jacobs, Piano: Carter 'Night Fantasies' (N. Y. Premiere)," *High Fidelity-Musical America* 32 (March 1982):MA 28.

Bayan Northcott, "Brev fra London," *Dansk Musiktidsskrift* 55, no. 3 (1980):131.

Charles Rosen, Liner notes for recording of "Night Fantasies" and Sonata; performed by Rosen. Etcetera Records 1008.

David Schiff, "Musical Time in Elliott Carter's 'Night Fantasies'," *Arnold Schoenberg Institute Elliott Carter Festival* (Spring 1983):4-7, 21-22.

Piano Concerto

Mark Blechner, "New York Philharmonic: Carter Piano Concerto," *High Fidelity-Musical America* 29 (March 1979):MA 22.

Benjamin Boretz, *The Nation* 204 (April 1967):445-46.

M. Bowen, *Music and Musicians* 18 (May 1970):60-61.

W. Burde, *Neue Zeitschrift für Musik* 130 (April 1969):167-68.

_____ *Orchester* 17 (May 1969):211-12.

Cleveland Orchestra (December 1969):435-45.

Arthur Cohn, "Elliott Carter's Piano Concerto," *American Record Guide* 34, no. 10 (June 1968):936.

Ronald Crichton, *Financial Times* (March 26, 1970).

S. Emmerson, "Carter and Davies," *Music and Musicians* 26 (August 1978):32-33.

Robert Finn, *Cleveland Plain Dealer* (December 14, 1969).

Edward Greenfield, *The Guardian* (March 26, 1970).

David Hamilton, "The New Craft of the Contemporary Concerto: Carter and Sessions," *High Fidelity* 18, no. 5 (May 1968):67-68.

Peter Heyworth, *The Observer Review* (March 29, 1970).

Leighton Kerner, "Carter's Fire-Eating Landmark," *Village Voice* (March 17, 1975).

Howard Klein, *New York Times* (March 17, 1968).

Irving Kolodin, *Saturday Review* 50 (February 11, 1967):85.

"Little to Think About," *Daily Express* (March 26, 1970).

Colin Mason, *Daily Telegraph* (March 26, 1970).

J. Meyerwitz, *Musica* 21 (1967):176.

John Meyer Perth, "The Idea of Conflict in the Concerto," *Studies in Musicology* 8 (1974):38-52.

Hubert Saal, *Newsweek* 69, no. 3 (January 16, 1967):94.

D. Shawe-Taylor, *American Musical Digest* 1, no. 6 (1970):14.

Michael Steinberg, *Boston Globe* (January 7, 1968).

_____ *High Fidelity-Musical America* 17 (May 1967):MA 16.

Kurt Stone, "Current Chronicle: New York," *Musical Quarterly* 55, no. 4 (October 1969).

H. H. Stuckenschmidt, *Melos* 36 (March 1969):122-23.

"Treat Worth the Travail," *Time* 89, no. 2 (January 13, 1967):44.

Stephen Walsh, "Elliott Carter's Piano Concerto," *The Listener* 81, no. 2087 (March 31, 1969):357.

_____ *The Times* (London) (March 6, 1970).

Piano Sonata

Robert Below, *Music Review* 34, no. 3-4 (1973):282-93.

Arthur Berger, *New York Herald Tribune* (May 3, 1948).

_____ "King David and Reforestation," *Saturday Review* 35, no. 13 (March 29, 1952):48.

_____ *New York Herald Tribune* (October 28, 1958).

Arthur Cohn, *American Record Guide* 29, no. 11 (July 1963):867-68.

Carter Harmon, *New York Times* (March 13, 1948).

_____ *New York Times* (May 3, 1948).

Ivor Keys, *Music and Letters* 30, no. 1 (January 1949):89.

E. H. W. Meyerstein, *Music Review* 10, no. 1 (February 1949):45.

Francis D. Perkins, *New York Herald Tribune* (March 6, 1947).

Charles Rosen, *Piano Sonata* performed by Charles Rosen. Liner notes on cover. Epic LC 3850.

Donald S. Steinfirst, *Pittsburgh Post Gazette* (December 18, 1947).

Noel Strauss, *New York Times* (March 6, 1947).

Virgil Thomson, *New York Herald Tribune* (March 13, 1948).

Pocahontas (Ballet)

John Martin, *New York Times* (May 25, 1939).

Sonata for Flute, Oboe, Cello and Harpsichord

O. Daniel, *Saturday Review* 43 (December 17, 1960):43.

David W. Moore, *The American Record Guide* 36, no. 7 (March 1970):498.

Eric Salzman, *New York Times* (July 23, 1961).

Virgil Thomson, *New York Herald Tribune* (November 11, 1953).

Lester Trimble, *Stereo Review* 24, no. 3 (March 1970):86-87.

Sonata for Violoncello and Piano
Arthur Berger, *New York Herald Tribune* (February 28, 1950).
———— "King David and Reforestation," *Saturday Review* 35, no. 13 (March 29, 1952):48.
William Bergsma, *Notes* 11, no. 3 (June 1954):434-35.
Louis Biancolli, *New York Sun* (February 28, 1950).
Miles Kastendieck, *New York Journal American* (February 28, 1950).
David W. Moore, *The American Record Guide* 36, no. 7 (March 1970):498.
Robert P. Morgan, *High Fidelity* 20, no. 2 (February 1970):84.
Virgil Thomson, *New York Herald Tribune* (November 20, 1950).

String Quartet No. 1
H. L. De la Grange, *Arts* (Paris) (November 5, 1957).
Edward Downes, *New York Times* (December 9, 1956).
Alfred Frankenstein, *San Francisco Chronicle* (January 6, 1956).
William Glock, *Encounter* 2, no. 6 (June 1954):60-63.
Max Harrison, *The Times* (London) (January 22, 1972).
Joseph Kerman, *Hudson Review* 11, no. 3 (Autumn 1958):420-25.
Irving Kolodin, *Saturday Review* 53, no. 18 (May 2, 1970):28.
Paul Henry Lang, *New York Herald Tribune* (October 24, 1958).
Martin Mayer, *Esquire* 47, no. 2 (February 1957):17.
Robert P. Morgan, *Musical Newsletter* 4, no. 3 (Summer 1974):3-11.
———— *High Fidelity* 21, no. 2 (February 1971):76-78.
George Rochberg, *Musical Quarterly* 43, no. 1 (January 1957):130-32.
D. Rodadinova, *Sovetskaya Muzyka* 36 (October 1972):84-87.
Harold Schonberg, *New York Times* (February 27, 1953).
Desmond Shawe-Taylor, *New Statesman and Nation* 50, no. 1290 (November 26, 1955):702-3.
Irving Soblovsky, *Chicago Daily News* (February 7, 1957).
Theodore M. Strongin, *New York Herald Tribune* (February 27, 1953).
Virgil Thomson, *New York Herald Tribune* (May 5, 1953).
Peter Yates, *Arts and Architecture* 76, no. 8 (August 1959):4-5, 8-10.

String Quartet No. 2
S. Bayliss, *Musical Times* 101 (June 1960):373.
A. Clements, "Composer's Quartet," *Music and Musicians* 25 (December 1976):51-52.
P. Dickenson, *Musical Times* 101 (June 1960):377.
R. W. Dumm, *Musical Courier* 162 (September 1960):14.
R. F. Goldman, *Musical Quarterly* 46, no. 3 (1960):361-64.
D. Hamilton, *High Fidelity-Musical America* 24 (July 1974):73-75.
Max Harrison, *The Times* (London) (January 22, 1972).
Irving Kolodin, *Saturday Review* 53, no. 18 (May 2, 1970):28.
Paul Henry Lang, *New York Herald Tribune* (March 26, 1960).
R. Moevs, *Musical Quarterly* 61 (1975):165-68.

Robert P. Morgan, *High Fidelity* 21, no. 2 (February 1971):76-78.
_____ *Musical Newsletter* 4, no. 3 (Summer 1974):3-11.
Ross Parmenter, *New York Times* (December 22, 1960).
Francis D. Perkins, *New York Herald Tribune* (December 22, 1960).
S. Sadie, *Musical Times* 110 (January 1969):52.
Eric Salzman, *New York Times* (May 7, 1961).
Harold Schonberg, *New York Times* (January 25, 1962).
Michael Steinberg, *Boston Globe* (December 4, 1968).
_____ *Melos* 28, no. 2 (February 1961):35-37.
_____ *Score*, no. 27 (July 1960):22-26.
Howard Taubman, *New York Times* (March 26, 1960).
_____ *New York Times* (April 3, 1960).

String Quartet No. 3
Byron Belt, *Newark Star-Ledger* (January 24, 1973).
William Bender, *Time* 101, no. 6 (February 5, 1973):59-60.
"Elliott Carter drittes Streichquartett," *Neue Zuericher Zeitung* (February 10, 1973).
D. Hamilton, "The Unique Imagination of Elliott Carter," *High Fidelity-Musical America* 25 (July 1974):73-75.
David Hamilton, *The Nation* 216 (February 19, 1973):250-52.
Donal Henahan, *New York Times* (January 25, 1973).
Harriet Johnson, *New York Post* (January 25, 1973).
P. Jones, "Rutgers University: Elliott Carter Lectures," *Current Musicology* 20 (1975):9–10.
Leighton Kerner, *Village Voice* (February 1, 1973).
Irving Kolodin, *Saturday Review of Education* 1, no. 2 (March 1973):80.
Martin Mayer, "Recordings," *Esquire* (August 1974):30.
R. Moevs, *Musical Quarterly* 61 (1975):165-68.
Robert P. Morgan, *Musical Newsletter* 4, no. 3 (Summer 1974):3-11.
J. Nagley, "String Quartets," *Musical Times* 123 (April 1982):277.
Nuova Revista Musicale 7, no. 2 (1973):266-70.
Andrew Porter, *New Yorker* 48, no. 50 (February 3, 1973):82-87.
J. Rockwell, *Music and Musicians* 21 (1973):58-59.
Patrick J. Smith, *High Fidelity-Musical America* 23, no. 4 (May 1973):MA 16.
Michael Steinberg, *Boston Globe* (February 11, 1973).
_____ *Boston Globe* (February 19, 1973).

Suite from the Minotaur
Douglas Watt, *New Yorker* 32, no. 14 (May 26, 1956).

Suite from Pocahontas
Arthur Cohn, *American Record Guide* 29, no. 11 (July 1963):867-68.

Charles Rosen, *Suite from Pocahontas* performed by the Zurich Radio Orchestra, Jacques Monod, conductor. Liner notes on cover. EPIC LC 3850.

Symphony No. 1
Eric Salzman, *New York Times* (July 23, 1961).
Paul Snook, *Fanfare* 6, no. 3 (January–February 1983):132-34.
John R. White, *Notes* 22, no. 1 (Fall 1965):820-21.

Symphony of Three Orchestras
R. Breuer, "Neues bei den New Yorker Philharmonikern," *Oesterreichische Musik Zeitschrift* 32 (May–June 1977):277-78.
J. W. Freeman, "Da New York," *Nuova Revista Musicale Italiana* 11, no. 2 (1977):251-53.
David Hamilton, "Elliott Carter's Contributions to the American Bicentennial," *High Fidelity-Musical America* 31 (August 1981):52.
David Harvey, *Tempo,* no. 143 (December 1982):30-31.
Leighton Kerner, "Elliott Carter Restores the Symphony's Double Identity," *Village Voice* (March 7, 1977):52.
Irving Kolodin, "Carter's Symphony: Beethoven by Maazel," *Saturday Review* 4 (April 2, 1977):37-38.
Max Loppert, "Carter's Symphony," *Financial Times* (March 23, 1979).
Andrew Porter, "Great Bridge, Our Myth," *New Yorker* 53 (March 7, 1977):101-4.
Gregory Sandow, "Music: Fed Up," *Village Voice* 26 (December 2, 1981):94.
Brigitte Schiffer, "Paris," *Music and Musicians* 26 (February 1978):53-54.
P. J. Smith, "New York," *Musical Times* 118 (April 1977):329.
R. Thackeray, "Orchestral," *Musical Times* 120 (May 1979):419.

Syringa
Marshall Bialosky, *Notes* 39, no. 4 (June 1983):957-59.
John Ditsky, *Fanfare* 6, no. 3 (January–February 1983):134.
Lawrence Kramer, " 'Syringa': John Ashbery and Elliott Carter," *Beyond Amazement: New Essays on John Ashbery,* ed. David Lehman (Ithaca: Cornell University Press, 1980), pp. 255-71.
Bayan Northcott, "Carter's 'Syringa'," *Tempo,* no. 128 (March 1979):31-32.
Andrew Porter, "Famous Orpheus," *New Yorker* (January 8, 1979):56-58, 61-63.
David Schiff, "Carter in the Seventies," *Tempo,* no. 130 (September 1979):2-10.

To Music
Henry Woodward, *Notes* 13, no. 2 (March 1956):348.

Triple Duo
Andrew Porter, "Thought-Executing Fires," *New Yorker* (May 9, 1983):114-18.

Variations for Orchestra
Alfred Frankenstein, *San Francisco Chronicle* (February 1, 1963).
Peter Heyworth, *The Observer Weekend Review* (August 28, 1966).
Nicholas Kenyon, *Music and Musicians* 25, no. 9 (May 1977):47.
Eugene Lees, *Louisville Times* (April 23, 1956).
Robert C. Marsh, *Chicago Sun-Times* (October 15, 1971).
Orin Moe, "The Music of Elliott Carter," *College Music Symposium* 22, no. 1 (Spring 1982):7-31.
Edwin H. Schloss, *Philadelphia Inquirer* (December 7, 1962).
Michael Steinberg, *Boston Globe* (March 20, 1964).
R. Stewart, "Serial Aspects of Elliott Carter's Variations for Orchestra," *Music Review* 34, no. 1 (1973):62-65.
Gillian Widdicombe, *Financial Times* (March 16, 1972).

Woodwind Quintet
Arthur Berger, *New York Herald Tribune* (October 24, 1949).
Oliver Daniel, *Bulletin of American Composers Alliance* 4, no. 2 (1954):21.
Carter Harmon, *New York Times* (February 28, 1949).
Virgil Thomson, *New York Herald Tribune* (February 28, 1949).

Dissertations

Daniel F. Breedon, "An Investigation of the Influence of the Metaphysics of Alfred North Whitehead upon the Formal Dramatic Compositional Procedure of Elliott Carter." D.M.A. diss., University of Washington, 1975.
Frederick D. Geissler, "Considerations of Tempo as a Structural Basis in Selected Orchestral Works of Elliott Carter." D.M.A. diss., Cornell, 1974.
Irene R. Grau, "Compositional Techniques Employed in the First Movement of Elliott Carter's Piano Concerto." Ph.D. diss., University of Rochester, 1975.
Samuel Philip Headrick, "Thematic Elements in the Variations Movement of Elliott Carter's String Quartet Number One." Ph.D. diss., University of Rochester, Eastman School of Music, 1981.
J. D. Jenny, "Elliott Carter: The Manipulation of Musical Time." D.M.A. diss., Ohio State University, 1979.
Mary Jane Kuchenmeister, "Formal and Thematic Relationships in the First String Quartet of Elliott Carter." M.M. thesis, University of Arizona, 1967.

William Wiley McElroy, "Elliott Carter's String Quartet No. 1: A Study of Heterogeneous Rhythmic Elements." M.M. thesis, Florida State University, 1973.

Eugene W. Schweitzer, "Generation in the String Quartets of Carter, Sessions, Kirchner, and Schuller." Ph.D. diss., University of Rochester, 1965.

Randall A. Shinn, "An Analysis of Elliott Carter's Sonata for Flute, Oboe, Cello, and Harpsichord." D.M.A. diss., University of Illinois, Urbana-Champaign, 1975.

D. A. Stein, "The Function of Pitch in Elliott Carter's 'String Quartet No. 1'." Ph.D. diss., Washington University, 1981.

Carmen Irene Wilhite, "Piano Sonata by Elliott Carter: A Foreshadowing of His Later Style: A Lecture Recital, Together with Three Recitals of Selected Works." D.M.A. diss., North Texas State University, 1977.

Francis R. Wyatt, "The Mid-20th Century Orchestral Variation, 1953-63: An Analysis and Comparison of Selected Works by Major Composers." Ph.D. diss., University of Rochester, Eastman School of Music, 1974.

About Charles Rosen

Born in New York City, Charles Rosen had by the age of four begun to pick out tunes he heard his mother practicing. His parents enrolled him at the Juilliard School of Music when he was six. At eleven Mr. Rosen left Juilliard to study with Moritz Rosenthal, a pupil of Liszt's, and with Rosenthal's wife Hedwig Kanner, a pupil of Leschetizky's. In 1951, the year he completed his doctoral work, Mr. Rosen made his New York debut, launching his performing career.

Charles Rosen is internationally renowned as a concert pianist and as a writer in the field of music history and analysis. He has appeared in concerts throughout the world. His extensive discography includes works by Bartók, Beethoven, Brahms, Chopin, Debussy, Haydn, Liszt, Mozart, Ravel, Scarlatti, Schoenberg, Schubert, and Schumann. Igor Stravinsky, Pierre Boulez, and Elliott Carter asked Mr. Rosen to record their works, and with Isaac Stern, Heather Harper, and Gregor Piatigorsky, he recorded the complete works of Anton Webern. Among his most recent recordings are his performance of Beethoven's *Diabelli Variations* (for which he received a Grammy Award nomination), a Schumann album, and Elliott Carter's *Night Fantasies* and Piano Sonata.

Mr. Rosen also has a Ph.D. in French literature from Princeton University and honorary doctorates from Trinity College, Dublin, and the Universities of Leeds and Durham in England. In 1971 he won a National Book Award for *The Classical Style: Haydn, Mozart, Beethoven* and is also the author of *Arnold Schoenberg and Music* and *Sonata Forms*. He has given the Ernest Bloch lectures at the University of California and was appointed to the Charles Eliot Norton Chair at Harvard University for 1980-81. He currently teaches at the State University of New York at Stony Brook and regularly contributes articles to the *New York Review of Books*.

☆ U.S. GOVERNMENT PRINTING OFFICE : 1984 O - 418-441 : QL 3

DUE